THE FILMS OF
WOODY
ALLEN

THE FILMS OF
WOODY ALLEN

Neil Sinyard

Exeter Books

NEW YORK

A Bison Book

Page 1:
Woody Allen: the face of modern comedy.

Pages 2–3:
The romantic Woody Allen, silhouetted
with Diane Keaton against
a Manhattan skyline in *Manhattan.*

Above:
Woody Allen's most dramatic screen role
to date: as the man fronting
for blacklisted writers in *The Front.*

CONTENTS

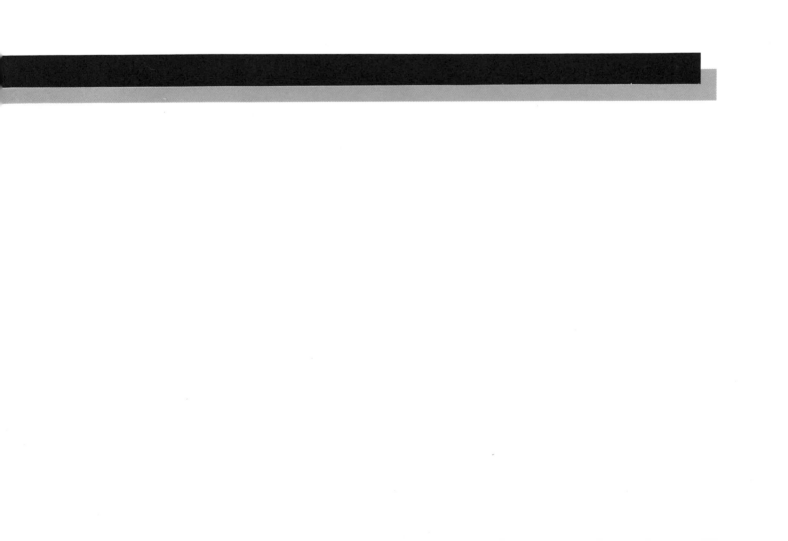

INTRODUCTION

WHINER TAKES ALL

Page 6: Woody Allen and Diane Keaton in *Play It Again, Sam.*

Woody Allen is the most original and brilliant screen comic since Charles Chaplin. His persona of the weakling worry-bead of modern society has become almost as instantly and internationally recognizable as Chaplin's Tramp: notice the chuckle of recognition that goes through every audience on his first appearance in *Hannah and Her Sisters* (1986). Like Chaplin, he is writer, director, star (when he chooses), sometimes even composer, and has achieved an artistic control rare in movies and almost unprecedented on any consistent basis in the American cinema. Like Chaplin, his comedies have an underlying seriousness and apprehension at the kind of hysteria and conformity of modern life that can harden into Fascism and McCarthyism – two evils that both Chaplin and Allen have attacked in their work.

However, whereas Chaplin paraded his social concern, Woody Allen parades his intellect. Whereas Chaplin's humor derives from his being a poet of poverty, Allen's derives from his being an artist of anxiety. Chaplin's comedy was a post-Victorian protest at the mechanization of man, but Allen's is a post-Freudian protest at the alienation of industrialized mass society. At the same time, Allen has made urban anxiety not only painful but funny and hence bearable. He has made sexual failure both poignant and hilarious.

Below: Bing Crosby (second from left) and Bob Hope (right) spar in *The Road to Morocco,* a favorite comedy of Allen, who has remained a great Hope fan.

Indeed he has sometimes had the audacity to stand the American Dream on its head, making movies about the emptiness of success and the nobility of failure, and yet without losing his audience.

Woody Allen's recurrent themes are sex and death ('It's not that I'm afraid to die, I just don't want to be around when it happens.') He wins over our sympathy because he faces these subjects not with a sentimental stoicism but with a believable, puckish panic; what one might call a grimace under pressure. He is sympathetic also because there is something endearing and unaggressive about his appearance and demeanor – his diminutive size, his ubiquitous spectacles, his world-weary red hair, his sad and anxious face. He is a whiner, not a smiler. In his case, whiner takes all.

As a comedian he has an astute sense of the absurd ('Did you hear about the streetwalker in Venice – who drowned?'); an adroit sense of juxtaposition ('Not only is there no God but try getting a plumber at weekends'), and an impeccable sense of timing in a sly tone of voice. He is a lovable outsider, a loser who is also a hero, vulnerable yet resilient. Yet generalizations about him are becoming increasingly difficult to sustain because of the extraordinary transformations ('development' is too weak a word) of his cinema over the last two decades, particularly in its increasing intellectual and technical ambitiousness. He has made quantum leaps between *farceur*, philosopher and fantasist in his films and is now not simply one of the great humorists of our time but one of its most formidable film-makers.

He was born Allen Stewart Konigsberg in Brooklyn in 1935, into a Jewish family, as he put it, 'dedicated to God and carpenting.' (Actually his father was at various times a jeweler, taxi-driver and waiter, and his mother was a book-keeper in a florist's shop.) No one has authoritatively explained nor assessed the significance of his change of name to Woody Allen. Perhaps, just as Eric Blair's assumption of the name of George Orwell was essentially prompted by his quest for a new identity, Allen wished to create a different image and personality for himself. Has he not said that his greatest wish is to be someone else? Yet the enigma remains. His films often seem autobiographical, yet the sardonic, streetwise persona of the movies is apparently nothing like the real man, who is serious, reclusive and so reserved that he preferred to play his clarinet in a New York night-club rather than face the razzmatazz of Los Angeles on Oscar night to collect his awards for *Annie Hall.*

Woody Allen fell in love with comedy when he saw Bob Hope in *The Road to Morocco* (1942). Encouraged by his schoolteachers, he began sending off gags and material to professional comics. Soon, in the company of Mel Brooks, Carl Reiner and Neil Simon, he was writing material for Sid Caesar shows, which set a standard for American television comedy that has never been surpassed. One thing stood out from this apprenticeship, however: his material seemed funnier when spoken by himself rather than delivered by

Left: Woody Allen's first screen role was in *What's New,Pussycat?* starring Peter O'Toole (center).

Left: Peter O'Toole (right) embraces his girlfriend Romy Schneider while Woody shyly unzips a suggestive banana in *What's New,Pussycat?*

other people. On that basis, his agents, Jack Rollins and Charles Joffe (later to become his trusted producers), persuaded a reluctant Woody to take his act into night-clubs and perform a comic monologue.

Woody Allen's stage act at this period has become famous through records (it was a great period for recorded American humor: the routines of comics like Shelley Berman, Bob Newhart, Alan Sherman, Mike Nichols and Elaine May were similarly and deservedly preserved). His night-club act has also been evoked and recalled in scenes in *Annie Hall* and *Broadway Danny Rose*. It is here that the persona of the shy failure and pint-sized Casanova were first perfected. The monologues were mock-autobiographical and generally directed against himself. His subjects included the privations of his early life (even his pet dog had a stammer); his family (a grandfather, who sold him his watch on his deathbed, a mother whom he fired as cleaner because she stole); and his first marriage (his wife was an immature woman who used to burst into the bathroom unannounced and sink all his boats). Encouraged by Shirley MacLaine to catch Woody's night-club act, producer Charles K Feldman was sufficiently impressed to commission a screenplay and also promise a small role for Woody for his film, *What's New, Pussycat?* (1965).

Above: More zany and sexy shenanigans in *What's New, Pussycat?*

Right: Woody plays his clarinet on *The Dick Cavett Show.*

Woody Allen has since spoken disparagingly of this movie, claiming that, 'If they had let me make it, I could have made it twice as funny and half as successful.' Warren Beatty was originally cast in the leading role, and Allen wanted Groucho Marx for the role of the analyst and a larger part for himself. In the event, Peter O'Toole took the part of the sex-obsessed magazine editor and Peter Sellers was his consulting psychiatrist, Fritz Fassbender. Despite Woody Allen's own dissatisfaction with it, the film remains a stylish and, for its time, surprisingly frank sex comedy, with intriguing hints of future Allen themes and traits: the difficulty of romantic love, the obsession with psychoanalysis, the impressive cultural allusions that range from Voltaire's *Candide* and Andrew Marvell's 'To His Coy Mistress' to Fellini's *8½* (1963). Feldman was also to cast Allen as James Bond's cousin in the jaded jape, *Casino Royale* (1967). By the end of the decade, he was becoming a bankable movie name, his credit undoubtedly increased by his play *Don't Drink the Water* (1969) also being brought to the screen by Howard Morris. In this, Jackie Gleason and Estelle Parsons head an American family vacationing abroad who land in the hostile country of Vulgaria and have to seek shelter in the political asylum of the American

Above: Woody Allen plays Jimmy Bond (nephew of James) in the spoof spy thriller, *Casino Royale.*

Left: Woody's Jimmy Bond seems shaken rather than stirred in this moment from *Casino Royale.*

11

Right: Estelle Parsons (left) and Jackie Gleason (center) play an ordinary American married couple caught up in continental politics in *Don't Drink the Water*, Howard Morris's version of Woody Allen's first stage success, a satire on spies and US diplomacy.

Above: Richard Libertini (left), as an eccentric priest, converses with Jackie Gleason (seated), as a harassed caterer, in *Don't Drink the Water*.

Embassy. Allen had no involvement in the film, though it featured two names on the technical credits who were to become important members of the Woody Allen team: producer Charles Joffe and editor Ralph Rosenblum.

However, Woody Allen's most eccentric encounter with the cinema at this stage came with the film, *What's Up, Tiger Lily?* (1966), originally a Japanese imitation of James Bond

entitled *Kizino Kizi* (director: Senkichi Taniguchi), and which Woody redubbed and re-edited. He even makes a couple of gnomic appearances himself, explaining that this sort of thing had all been done before in *Gone With the Wind* (1939) but refusing to explain the plot, which tells the story of the search for a missing egg salad recipe. The interest of the movie lies in its experimentation with film form, which seems to point to certain future

directions that Allen's own cinema will take. The disjunction between sight and sound – Japanese visuals dubbed into Brooklynese – will be similarly exploited in a scene in *Annie Hall*, where a conversation between hero and heroine is undermined and modified by subtitled thoughts that reveal completely different things on their minds. The strategy of superimposing one film on another anticipates *Zelig*. Woody Allen's sport, over the soundtrack and at the editing table, with film narrative in *What's Up, Tiger Lily?* is similar to the games with documentary that Orson Welles later played in *F for Fake* (1976). It is also a very funny film, punctuated by savage imprecations that one has previously only been able to guess at from Japanese movies – 'Saracen pig!' 'Spartan dog!' 'Roman cow!' 'Russian snake!' 'Spanish fly!' and so on. From *What's Up, Tiger Lily?* it was hard to tell whether Allen was a comic original or simply a transplant artist, but more orthodox evidence of talent was shortly to be forthcoming.

Left: Woody takes a nibble of an Oriental's apple in *What's Up, Tiger Lily?*

Below: The poster for *What's Up, Tiger Lily?*, Woody Allen's hilarious reworking of a Japanese thriller.

CHAPTER ONE

THE COMEDY OF INCOMPETENCE

1969-1975

Page 14: Woody Allen in *Sleeper.*

Woody Allen's early films are probably more highly regarded now than they were at the time. Even the Martian in *Stardust Memories* (1980) says he prefers the 'early, *funny*' films. Those critics who are suspicious of Allen's later development relish the free-wheeling absurdity of his output in this period. Also the coarsening in American comedy in the late 1970s and early 1980s – from National Lampoons to Porkys – makes these early movies, in retrospect, look even better.

At the time these films seemed to place Woody Allen in the Bob Hope tradition of film *farceur* with asides to the camera, games with movie plots and realism, and a hero who plays the role of cowardly braggart and great lover as a private joke between himself and the audience. Like Bob Hope's films, they could be described as comedy of incompetence. In *Play It Again, Sam*, Allen is a romantic incompetent; in *Take the Money and Run* (1969), a criminal incompetent.

In *Bananas* (1971), *Sleeper* (1973) and *Love and Death* (1975), Allen derives humor from

spoofs of familiar film forms, which cause a number of comparisons with a comic contemporary like Mel Brooks who sends up the western in *Blazing Saddles* (1974) and the horror film in *Young Frankenstein* (1974); indeed Brooks does not so much parody these forms as perform demented transplants on them. Gradually, a number of things become apparent which will distinguish Woody Allen from Mel Brooks, and they go deeper than S J Perelman's cruel distinction: 'the defining difference is that Allen is funny and Brooks is not.' Allen's movies become less joyously vulgar than Brooks's and more philosophically personal. Their movement is less toward farcical acrobatics than Freudian anxiety, and eventually Brooks's *oeuvre* as a companion piece to Allen's will be displaced by that of Ingmar Bergman.

Take the Money and Run (1969) was Allen's first important foray as actor, director and writer – in this case, co-writing the script with Mickey Rose, who later also collaborated on *Bananas.* Allen plays the role of Virgil

Below: Woody in a potentially explosive situation from *Take the Money and Run,* his directing debut.

Above: How not to hold up a bank: from *Take the Money and Run.*

Starkwell, social misfit and born failure. He is a bemused bank-robber who cannot even compose a legible hold-up note, the argument with a clerk over whether the word is 'Gun' or 'Gub' allowing a line to form behind him and eventually helping him to get arrested. Virgil's record of ineptitude is soon of awesome proportions: sixteen banks, sixteen convictions.

What set him off on this life of crime? His early story is narrated in fulsome 'March of Time' tones by Jackson Beck. This gives Allen an opportunity to compose some pastiche newsreel footage (an intriguing anticipation of his much more sophisticated elaboration of this technique in *Zelig*) and to parody the documentary pretensions of a number of recent gangster movies, notably Arthur Penn's *Bonnie and Clyde* (1967) and Roger Corman's *The St Valentine's Day Massacre* (1967). Through interviews with his parents hideously over-disguised in false mustaches and giant spectacles to hide their shame (to the extent that Virgil's mother

looks like Groucho Marx), we learn of Virgil's hapless beginnings in crime as a timid knife-man and pool-hustler. Apparently an attempt to rob a local pet shop was foiled when Virgil was chased away by a gorilla. He began stealing, it seems, in order to pay for his cello lessons, though as his music teacher comments: 'He had no conception of the instrument – he was blowing into it.'

Virgil takes over the narration when he meets a girl, Louise (Janet Margolin). 'After fifteen minutes I wanted to marry her,' he says, 'and after half an hour I'd completely given up the idea of stealing her purse.' The following scene shows Virgil/Woody trying and failing to live up to a modern image of the romantic hero; displaying his puny torso as he trots around in a bath towel as a ditheringly diminutive macho man, and posturing so much in front of the mirror that only when he has left the room does he notice he has no trousers. He and Louise are married and a comically frenzied love scene follows, in which the only observable erotic objects are the couple's feet

Right: In *Take the Money and Run,* Woody's hero Virgil first takes to crime in order to pay for his cello lessons.

Far right: A publicity shot for *Bananas,* Woody Allen's superb satire on banana republics and political banana skins.

Below: Woody in love: Janet Margolin plays his wife in *Take the Money and Run.*

and Virgil's spectacles that end up on Louise. Needless to say, his criminal life puts a strain on his marriage, particularly when Louise takes a long time in the bathroom on the morning of a heist, which might make him late, and contrives to wash the wrong shirt ('I can't wear beige for a bank robbery!')

Take the Money and Run is rather splutteringly constructed, with the result that it just jumps from joke to joke rather than builds a narrative and comic momentum, yet the humor is so varied and enterprising that this matters less than expected. The dialogue is typically sharp and self-deprecating (explaining a failed mugging attempt on an old lady, Virgil has to confess that 'I got a hit in the groin with a crutch'). There are some eccentric visual jokes, as when Virgil works in the prison laundry and unaccountably turns up a bra. Much of the comedy derives from the mimicry of television shows and the sardonic scrutiny of film conventions. A job interview turns into an episode of 'What's My Line?' When two gangs arrive to rob a bank at the same time, the customers are invited to indicate by applause which gang they would prefer to be robbed by. When Virgil runs a film of the layout of the bank for his desperadoes, he insists on preceding his film show with a cartoon short ('Trout Fishing in Quebec'). His plan for the gang to pose as a film crew for the robbery is taken too seriously by Fritz (clearly modelled on Lang) who starts barking out Germanic orders.

Not all of the jokes work, largely because sometimes the idea is funnier than the visual form it takes (Virgil on a chain gang having to spend several days 'locked in a sweat box with an insurance salesman' is a joke that sounds better than it looks). At the same time, *Take the Money and Run* is a comedy of ideas, not

Above: A rebel has been bitten by a snake and needs a comrade to suck out the poison: Woody delightedly prepares to oblige. From *Bananas*.

Right: Woody struggles with a hand grenade in *Bananas*.

characterized the Marx Brothers' *Duck Soup* (1933). His romantic co-star this time is Louise Lasser, who appeared briefly in *Take the Money and Run* as one of the witnesses who thought Virgil too much of an idiot to be a famous criminal and who in real life, was Woody Allen's second wife (though they were shortly to be divorced). As in the first film, Marvin Hamlisch provides a bouncy score, and Ralph Rosenblum's editing gives a real slickness to this comedy about the political banana skins that are forever up-ending the rulers of a banana republic.

'Blood!' says Fielding Mellish (Woody Allen), feeling his head. 'That should be on the *inside*!' He has just made contact with Latin American rebels, his first step toward becoming a pint-sized Castro. Previously he has been a product tester for an American conglomerate, first seen demonstrating an exercising machine for the working executive which, rather like the food machine that attacks Chaplin in *Modern Times* (1936), goes madly out of control. Disappointed when his

simply a ramshackle collection of routines. Its use of witnesses to comment on Virgil, its gleeful absurdity in constructing bizarre family backgrounds for Virgil and Louise, are delicious jokes at the expense of the sociological content of gangster movies and at the pretensions of sociology generally. The film's variety of forms is not simply opportunistic but suggests the kind of cultural indoctrination that modern man is prone to – from TV shows, movies, the romantic fantasies exploited in advertising etc. This is a theme which will be elaborated more seriously in *Manhattan*. Mainly, though, the significance of the film is the establishment of Woody Allen's screen persona as the endearing loser. 'He never made the most wanted list,' complains Louise of Virgil, adding: 'it's unfair voting . . . it's who you know.'

If *Take the Money and Run* was a wild combination of Bob Hope and *Bonnie and Clyde*, Woody Allen's next movie *Bananas* (1971) was an equally bizarre mating of Chaplin and the Marx Brothers. It satirizes dictatorships in the manner of Chaplin's *The Great Dictator* (1940) and observes political revolution with the lunatic surrealism that

romance with a young political activist collapses, he wanders into an operating theater to tell his parents he is leaving New York for San Marcos, outraging his surgeon father to such an extent that he is compelled to finish his father's operation ('I'll finish this *one*,' Fielding concedes). In Latin America, a plan by the dictator to assassinate Fielding and win American aid by blaming it on the rebels goes awry, and Fielding not only falls into the hands of the rebels but eventually becomes their

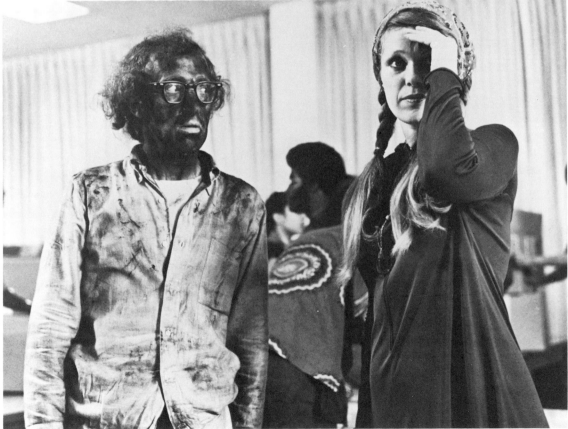

Above: Fielding Mellish (Woody Allen) returns to America in *Bananas*, in a disguise pitched between Fidel Castro and Groucho Marx.

Left: Woody as the hapless Fielding Mellish in *Bananas*, with Nancy (Louise Lasser) as his politically active girlfriend. Louise Lasser was Woody Allen's second wife.

leader. When he returns to America, he is arrested and put on trial.

As in *Take the Money and Run*, the jokes range widely in quality and style. A political prisoner in San Marcos is tortured by playing him the score of *Naughty Marietta* (there is a similar scene in Billy Wilder's 1961 political satire, *One, Two, Three*, where a Communist is tortured by the incessant playing of that ultimate example of capitalist decadence, 'Yellow Polka-Dot Bikini'). At the president's palace, Fielding is entertained by a mute, miming string quartet – by repute, an inspired improvisation on the part of the director when the instruments failed to turn up on time. (One is reminded of Orson Welles's brilliant staging of the murder of Roderigo in *Othello* in a Turkish bath when the actors' costumes failed to arrive.) Some of the jokes derive their humor from recognition of film quotation: a pram careers down some steps in the manner of the Odessa Steps sequence in

Above: Fielding Mellish pretends to read his copy of *Commentary*, as an old lady is mugged on the subway in *Bananas*. The mugger in the middle is Sylvester Stallone in his first screen role.

Right: Fielding displays some of his sexual problems in *Bananas*.

A JACK ROLLINS · CHARLES H. JOFFE Production

woody allen's
"bananas" AA

with LOUISE LASSER · Executive Producer CHARLES H. JOFFE · Produced by JACK GROSSBERG · Directed by WOODY ALLEN
Associate Producer and Editor RALPH ROSENBLUM, A.C.E. · Written by WOODY ALLEN and MICKEY ROSE · Music by MARVIN HAMLISCH · COLOUR by De Luxe® United Artists

Eisenstein's revolutionary movie, *Battleship Potemkin* (1925); an eating/seduction scene, with junk food, is a take-off of a famous scene in *Tom Jones* (1963). Occasionally they come from the comic's ability to exploit a convention or idea to its illogical absurdity: for example, Fielding's ordering of a takeaway meal for a thousand rebels; or his lyrical reverie when he is invited to dinner with the President, cut short when he discovers that the mood setting harpist is not simply on the soundtrack but in his hotel cupboard. The blackest joke is the pre-credit scene, where a political assassination is set up as a televised sporting spectacular, with commentary by Howard Cosell. It has something of the incongruous cheeriness of the apocalyptic denouement of Kubrick's *Dr Strangelove* (1963), but is also an uncomfortable comment on recent American history – political assassination as sport for live, primetime television.

The central comic set-piece is Fielding's trial. It is a scene which brings together a cluster of themes and stylistic characteristics of the movie but, at the same time, is so brilliant that it stands as an almost extractable sequence of the most cherishable comedy about the times. The witnesses include a glossily moronic Miss America and J Edgar Hoover disguised as a black housewife. The

trial is interrupted by a Perry Mason style confession by a man who then realizes he has wandered into the wrong courtroom, and the verdict is delayed by an interpolated commercial for New Testament cigarettes ('I smoke them' says the priest, '*He* smokes them'). Tasteless perhaps, but one should remember Woody Allen's own quoted comments about television at the time, 'a medium run by cretins to pander to the lowest taste of the American public.' In *Hannah and Her Sisters* the tirade of the artist, Frederick, against the unctuous preachers of American television is in a similar style.

During the trial, Fielding is bound and gagged but still manages to unnerve a shaky witness ('Don't put words in my mouth!') through his grunted, indecipherable questioning. Funny certainly, but also an overt allusion to the notorious contempt trial of the Chicago Ten in 1969, where one of the defendants, Bobby Seale, was similarly bound and gagged. There is no doubt that *Bananas* tunes in, both hilariously and provocatively, to recent events and characteristics of American political life – the Bay of Pigs fiasco, CIA machinations, slippery alliances, judicial farce – and, equally significantly, the film's total irreverence distances Allen himself from any specific political commitment or orientation.

Above: The poster for *Bananas*, conveying the madcap spirit of the film.

Above: Woody Allen plays a film critic obsessed by Humphrey Bogart in *Play It Again, Sam*, directed by Herbert Ross.

Significantly, Fielding Mellish is a hero for whom politics becomes an inadvertent substitute for social failure and disappointed love. Ultimately, Woody Allen is less an analyst of political alliances than of personal anxieties. At a session with his analyst, Fielding discloses that he stole a pornographic book in braille ('I rubbed the dirty parts') and also gives details of a strange dream in which two crucifixion processions (of which he is one of the victims) fight over a parking space. It is one of the many strange visionary sequences in Woody Allen, and the analyst scene focuses on the two central anxieties of Allen's forthcoming work: sex and death. In the trial scene, when Fielding crumples under his own cross-examination, one senses an anticipation of the taut self-analysis and nervous breakdown structure that will characterize *Stardust Memories*. Another curious intimation of the

adaptation of his successful stage play, *Play It Again, Sam* (1972), Woody Allen entrusted the direction to Herbert Ross, perhaps out of a desire to reflect a little more about screen direction, perhaps out of recognition of the different nature of the subject. In contrast to the previous two films, with their scatter-brained plots, fusillade of gags and multiple cinematic styles, *Play It Again, Sam* is a plot-oriented (rather than joke-oriented) piece. It is also his first film with Diane Keaton and a more overtly romantic and nostalgic work than earlier films, in which Woody adopts his most popular screen persona – that of a walking worry-bead.

Allen plays an insecure, divorced film critic, Allan Felix, who is sexually harassing himself and who invokes the ghost of Humphrey Bogart to restore his romantic self-confidence. In the process, he finds himself falling in love with the wife (Diane Keaton) of his best friend (Tony Roberts), which leads to a brief affair and then to a grand gesture of renunciation at a fog-bound airport in the

Below: Woody gets to play his *Casablanca* farewell scene in *Play It Again, Sam* with Diane Keaton.

Bottom: The real thing: 'Here's looking at you, kid,' says Humphrey Bogart to Ingrid Bergman in *Casablanca*, as they bid farewell at the airport.

future is that moment when a young Sylvester Stallone appears as a subway mugger, while Woody tries to hide unconcernedly behind his copy of *Commentary*. The cinema of the 1980s is foreshadowed in that shot: Stallone's cinema of slobbish violence (in *Bananas* ironically playing the kind of character he will annihilate so distastefully in *Cobra*) against Woody Allen's cinema of sophisticated satire.

For his next film, starring in his own

Above: Woody Allen and Diane Keaton in *Play It Again, Sam.* This was the beginning of their productive film association.

Right: Woody plays a diminutive he-man in *Play It Again, Sam.*

Far right: Laying Bogart's ghost: Woody beds his best friend's wife in *Play It Again, Sam,* a typically ambivalent moment in his films where romantic fulfillment is inseparable from emotional guilt.

manner of the last scene of the Bogart classic *Casablanca* (1943).

As in the previous films, *Play It Again, Sam* playfully mimics film styles – the wife fantasizing a revenge along the lines of Italian movie melodrama, the husband Dick committing a watery suicide in the manner of James Mason's fading film star in Cukor's *A Star is Born* (1954). The main laughs come through the macho materializations of Bogey's ghost,

nicely played by Jerry Lacy, and the comic contrast between the hero's self-image (neurotic, weak, lacking in confidence) and that of Bogart's existential man (cool, confident, self-contained).

If there is a serious sub-theme to the work, it is its suggestion of a relationship between fantasy and failure, and between nostalgia and neurosis. For the critic in *Play It Again, Sam,* movies are a temporary escape from his own tribulations but also a weird behavior model through which he believes his situation might be transformed. Allen's films are often about the tension between Art and Life, Fantasy and Reality (most obviously perhaps in *Stardust Memories* and *The Purple Rose of Cairo*). Movies might be simpler and more exciting than real life, but one must be able to distinguish between them. The moral vindication of the hero in *Play It Again, Sam* comes when he confesses that one of his lines is not his own but actually a quote from *Casablanca* – a moment when he admits and confronts his own private fantasies. 'You don't need me anymore,' Bogey tells him at the end, adding: 'Here's looking at *you*, kid.' Self-recognition and respect will become a recurring battle for the Woody Allen hero.

Play It Again, Sam encloses its serious themes in a cozy romantic comedy. It has a good basic idea which one of Woody Allen's future co-writers, Marshall Brickman, later borrowed for one of his own movies, *Lovesick* (1983), which attempts to do for Freud what Allen does for Bogart. In retrospect, however, the joke looks a little incongruous. One cannot imagine now that a Woody Allen character would see Humphrey Bogart as his

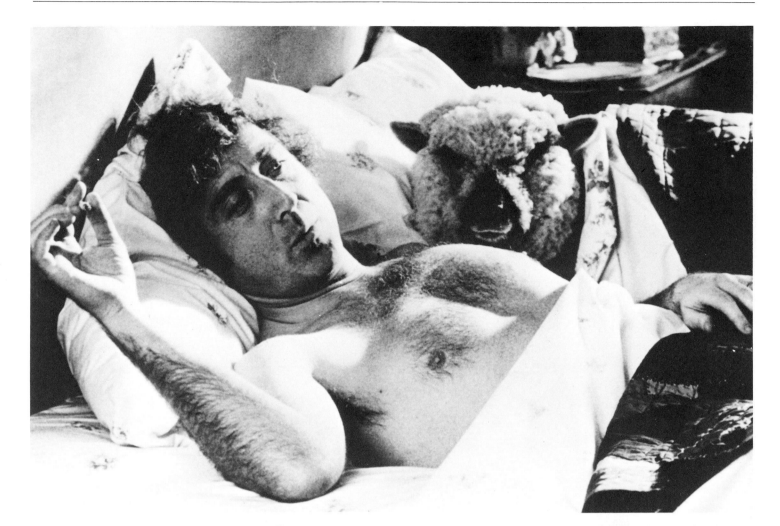

Above: Gene Wilder falls for a sheep in *Everything You Always Wanted to Know About Sex But Were Afraid to Ask.*

Right: Woody during an awkward encounter in *Everything You Always Wanted to Know About Sex . . .*

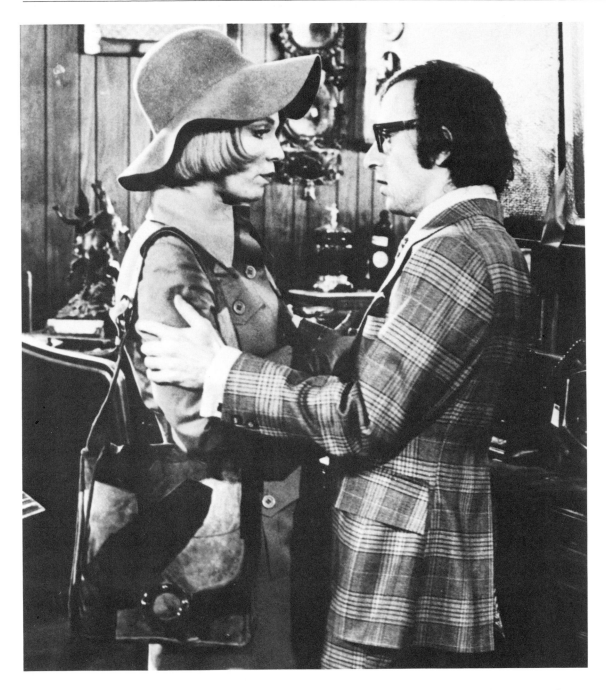

Left: Woody Allen and Louise Lasser in *Everything You Always Wanted to Know About Sex . . .*

ideal: it would more likely be Ingmar Bergman. Also Bogart was not essentially a romantic actor, which makes his role in the film seem as slightly askew as the misquotation in the title. Nevertheless, audiences obviously liked the extra warmth as well as the familiar wit which they found in *Play It Again, Sam*. It was Allen's most successful film since *What's New, Pussycat?*

In *Annie Hall*, Allen defines sex as 'the most fun I've ever had without laughing.' However, sex is truly a funny business in *Everything You Always Wanted to Know About Sex But Were Afraid to Ask* (1972), his film version of Dr David Reuben's best-selling sex manual. After *Play It Again, Sam*, Woody resumes the directing role and, in contrast to the conventional narrative structure of the preceding film, interprets Dr Reuben's book in a series of revue sketches on sexual

themes. 'The picture contains every funny idea that I've ever had about sex,' Woody has commented, 'including several that led to my divorce.'

Woody himself appears as a medieval court jester who would fain 'cop a feel' of the Queen's 'bare bodkin'; as a macho Italian husband, Fabrizio, with a frigid wife; as a man on the run from a giant breast that is terrorizing the countryside and can only be apprehended by a massive bra; and as a nervous sperm preparing for his space odyssey. In the other sketches, Lou Jacobi appears as a transvestite who scandalizes his in-laws when he reveals his frilly underwear; Gene Wilder falls in love with a sheep; and 'What's My Line?' is again parodied in a panel game called 'What's My Perversion?'

If *Take the Money and Run* was a satire on pop sociology, *Everything You Always Wanted*

Right: Woody as the court jester in the 'Do Aphrodisiacs Work?' sketch from *Everything You Always Wanted to Know About Sex . . .*

Below: Woody Allen plays Fabrizio who is having trouble with his frigid wife in *Everything You Always Wanted to Know About Sex . . .* Louise Lasser is made up to look like Monica Vitti in this pointed satire on Italian alienation.

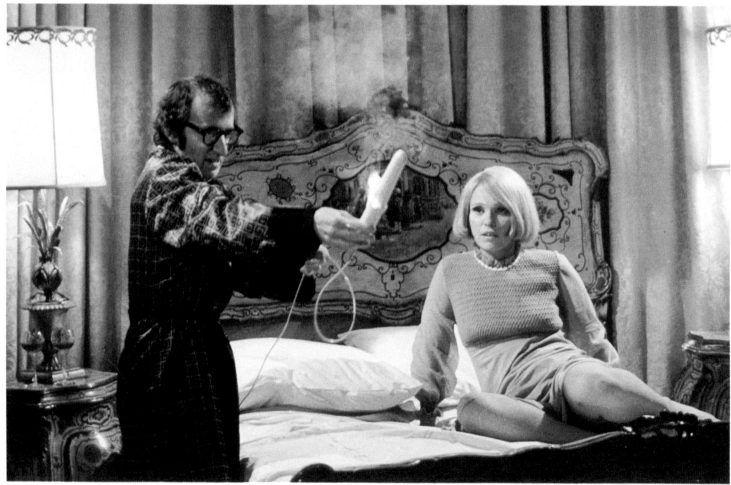

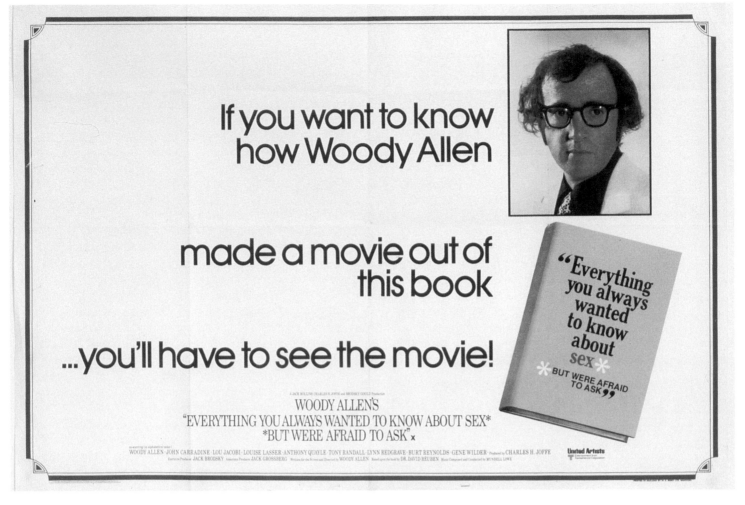

If you want to know how Woody Allen

made a movie out of this book

...you'll have to see the movie!

A JACK ROLLINS-CHARLES H. JOFFE and BRODSKY-GOULD Production

WOODY ALLEN'S
"EVERYTHING YOU ALWAYS WANTED TO KNOW ABOUT SEX*
*BUT WERE AFRAID TO ASK" x

co-starring (in alphabetical order)
WOODY ALLEN · JOHN CARRADINE · LOU JACOBI · LOUISE LASSER · ANTHONY QUAYLE · TONY RANDALL · LYNN REDGRAVE · BURT REYNOLDS · GENE WILDER · Produced by CHARLES H. JOFFE
Executive Producer JACK BRODSKY · Associate Producer JACK GROSSBERG · Written for the Screen and Directed by WOODY ALLEN · Based upon the book by DR. DAVID REUBEN · Music Composed and Conducted by MUNDELL LOWE

United Artists

to Know About Sex ... pokes fun now at pop
sexual psychology. As usual in Woody Allen at
this time it treats genuine emotional anxieties
with a saucy and satirical frankness. Some of
the jokes hardly get off the Freudian couch.
The revue sketch format might have seemed
a way of getting around Allen's difficulty with
narrative at that time. However, once the
basis of the joke has been established, the
danger is one of repetition with variation,
rather than a genuine development of hilarity.
Intriguingly some critics were later to attack
Zelig and *The Purple Rose of Cairo* on similar
grounds, as being feature length elaborations
of single joke ideas, but, by that time, the
issue had become much more complex and
contentious. Also, by that late stage Allen's
movies had become much more elaborate and
interesting visually. In *Everything* ... the
camera work and design are still fairly func-
tional, apart from the wittily weird sets in the
Italian sketch to evoke a sense of alienation in
the manner of Antonioni.

The best episodes are the ones either with
the strongest narrative structure, or in which
Allen himself takes the most important role,
or both. Gene Wilder's love for the sheep in
the bestiality sketch works because the love
affair is the most fully developed relationship
in the picture, and because it is underpinned

by a parody of William Wyler's *Carrie* (1952) –
with Wilder in the Laurence Olivier role and
the sheep playing Jennifer Jones. In 'Do
Aphrodisiacs Work?' Allen builds a likeable
portrait of a struggling clown, haplessly
caught up in a variation of *Hamlet* ('TB or not
TB,' he muses, 'consumption be done about
it?') His plot to seduce the Queen by slipping
an aphrodisiac into her goblet (on which there
is a deposit) is foiled by her fearsome chastity

Top: The poster for
*Everything You Always
Wanted to Know About
Sex . . .*

Above: Woody is chased by
a gigantic breast in
*Everything You Always
Wanted to Know About
Sex . . .*

31

belt. 'I must think of something quickly' wails the clown, 'because before you know it the Renaissance will be here and we'll all be painting.' In the 'What Happens During Ejaculation' sketch the inside of a man's body is conceived of as a massive space station and Woody toils beneath the surface as an industrious but worried sperm ('You hear rumors about the pill these women take'). It is a clever idea which somehow manages to unite two of Allen's favorite humorous targets – *Metropolis* and masturbation – into a single comic concept.

Woody Allen's next film, *Sleeper* (1973) was to take the sci-fi elements of *Everything You Always Wanted to Know About Sex* and elaborate them into a complete feature. The co-owner of the Happy Carrot Health Food store in Greenwich Village, Miles Monroe (Allen), after a routine operation, awakens two centuries later into a totalitarian America. 'I knew it was too good to be true,' he cries, 'I parked right near the hospital!' As in

Bananas, he is reluctantly coerced into joining a resistance movement ('I'm not the heroic type, I was beaten up by Quakers'). At different times this requires him to impersonate a domestic robot and to steal the dictator's nose, all that remains of the leader after a bomb attack.

Sleeper is more unified, more visually comic than his preceding movies, even if it lacks their explosive flashes of ingenious absurdity. In a way, the sci-fi trappings allow Woody to coast along on the genre's distinguished antecedents with irreverent comic reference, with bits of *Fahrenheit 451* (the bland TV-dominated society), *Brave New World* (the depersonalized sexual freedom) and *2001* (the computer in the operating theater). Woody himself is variously Rip Van Winkle, Gulliver in a gigantic world (slipping on a mountainous banana skin and braining an enemy with a monstrous strawberry) and, in one glorious moment, Tennessee Williams's Blanche du-Bois, depending on the kindness of strangers. The antics are sharpened by Allen's own jazzy score that matches the movie's own swinging, improvisatory rhythms.

One of the basic comic conceits behind *Sleeper* is to reveal the absurdity of modern life through speculating what it might look like from the vantage point of the year 2173. The modern fad for health foods is satirized by the doctors' amazement at Miles's preference for wheatgerm and organic honey over cream pies, steak, hot fudge and tobacco. (We notice that McDonald's is still flourishing in this futuristic society.) By the same token, when Miles is invited to comment on some curious artefacts of the earlier society, it permits Woody Allen to make some pithy remarks about facets and faces of our society, from the dubious delights of boxing as a sport to Billy Graham ('he knew God personally . . . they went out on double dates together') and Norman Mailer ('he donated his ego to Harvard Medical School'). His astringent comments on political leaders such as Stalin and Nixon do not reveal any surprises, other than a predictable distrust of political wisdom and solutions. (Later in the film he says that he does not believe either in science or God: the realities of life for him remain sex and death.) The underlying joke of the sequence is the specter it raises about the reliability of oral history – will the new society really believe Miles when he describes Bela Lugosi as the Mayor of New York and Charles de Gaulle as a French chef?

Another source of humor arises from the contrast between Miles's extraordinary situation and his mundane and materialist reaction to it. Wake him up two centuries later and his first thought is that his rent is over two

Below: Miles Monroe (Woody Allen) makes his escape from the security forces in the totalitarian society of *Sleeper.*

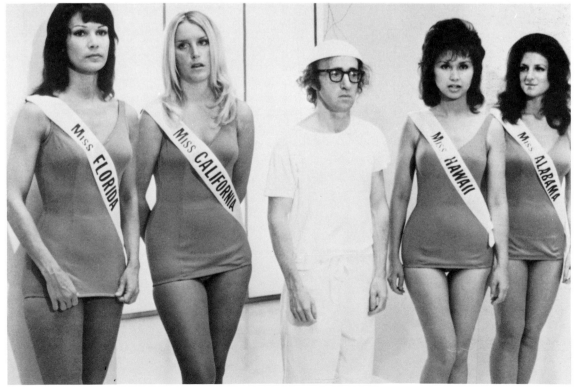

Above: On the run and disguised as a robot, Woody helps to make a house party go with a swing in *Sleeper*.

Left: The beauty contest in *Sleeper*, with Woody (center) as an outsider.

Far right: Woody's inflated hero escapes across land and sea in *Sleeper.*

Right: Diane Keaton plays Luna, the reluctant ally of Woody's reluctant rebel in *Sleeper.*

Below: Woody Allen plays Miles Monroe in *Sleeper,* the owner of a health food restaurant who awakens two hundred years later after a routine operation.

thousand months overdue. The film is generally at its funniest when the plot is standing still and our hero is responding maniacally to his predicament as in the scene where, disguised as a robotic servant in a futuristic kitchen, he makes an instant pudding that turns suddenly into The Blob. It is less funny when Miles is feeding plot lines rather than comic lines into the narrative mechanism.

The second half of *Sleeper* is basically a chase plot, with a seasoning of romance as Miles becomes involved with Luna (Diane Keaton) and some visual evocations of what trips to the tailors or to the confessional might be like in two centuries time. Although Woody exhibits more slapstick skills than one had previously witnessed (whether in flight, dangling Harold Lloyd style from a ladder, or simply doing his mechanical shuffle as the robot), the film tends to run out of surprises. At this stage in his career, one senses a tension between his skill as a stand-up comic and cinema as a narrative medium, and between the forms of his films and their underlying philosophy (is a sci-fi spoof really the best vehicle in which to carry Woody's thoughts about modern life and the problems of existence?) His next film would reveal similar tensions but it would also hint at some possible solutions.

On the surface, *Love and Death* (1975) seems to continue some of the comic strategies of *Sleeper*. Whereas *Sleeper* unleashed Woody's contemporary comic persona in a futuristic society, *Love and Death* places him in 1812 Russia as a 'militant coward', Boris, who is persuaded by his wife Sonia (Diane Keaton) to try and assassinate Napoleon. Just as *Sleeper* lets Woody loose inside science fiction, *Love and Death* lets him loose inside costume epic. One might be forgiven for thinking at this stage that this was to be the main idea behind Woody Allen's future work: that is, allowing a wisecracking New York Jewish intellectual to wander through and comment on the traditional film genres – the western, the gangster, the musical, and so on. As it happens, he moves less in the direction of movie pastiche than of personalized essay and, in its balance between these two modes, *Love and Death* is an important transitional work.

The immediate cultural inspiration behind *Love and Death* is, of course, the Russian novel of the nineteenth century and, specifically Tolstoy's *War and Peace*. (Intriguingly, Tolstoy will be quoted in an important context in *Hannah and Her Sisters*: 'The only absolute knowledge attainable by man is that life is meaningless'.) Woody Allen's Boris is the equivalent of Tolstoy's poet-pacifist Pierre: he will similarly be involved in a duel, will similarly attempt to kill the French Emperor. Dostoevsky is also cited in a funny scene between Boris and his father where a bit of gossip they share about one of their neighbors, Raskolnikov, (hero of *Crime and Punishment*) develops into an exchange of Dostoevsky book titles – Raskolnikov being a raw youth who must have been an 'idiot' to become so 'possessed' etc. The Dostoevsky references are carried a little further, in fact. In real life, Dostoevsky was sentenced to death and pardoned minutes before his execution. In *Love and Death*, Boris is expecting the same thing to happen to him, for he has been

Below: Boris slips into someone more comfortable (Olga Georges-Picot). A daring midnight tryst in *Love and Death.*

visited in his death cell by an Angel who promises a pardon ('Then there is a God,' cries Boris, before going into an impromptu reverential cadenza: 'And he shall dwell in the House of God . . . for six months . . . with an option to buy . . .'). In fact, a disconsolate Boris, standing by the Grim Reaper, will have to admit later that: 'I got screwed . . .'

The cultural references extend to the cinema – significantly, the art cinema, an indication that he is beginning to move filmically upmarket to a more specialized audience, with the sophistication more on display. Allen's use of music by Prokofiev, notably Prokofiev's score for *Alexander Nevsky*, anticipates the use of Mendelssohn's music in *A Midsummer Night's Sex Comedy* (1982); reminds us that Prokofiev wrote an opera based on *War and Peace*; and is also a reminder of Prokofiev's association with

Above: Boris goes for a stroll with the Grim Reaper in *Love and Death.*

Eisenstein, whose montage theories are mockingly employed in *Love and Death*. The stone lions that rear up at the slaughter of innocents in Eisenstein's *Battleship Potemkin* flop down in sexual exhaustion in Allen's *Love and Death* after a night of love between Boris and Sonia. When the generals from afar watch their soldiers charging into battle, Allen inserts a shot of a flock of sheep to convey their real impression of their men – a nice deployment of Eisenstein's and Pudovkin's experiments with the metaphoric potential of montage in the 1920s.

The main cinematic influence in *Love and Death*, however, is Ingmar Bergman, the first time he has appeared as such a potent presence in a Woody Allen movie (as we shall see, from now on, Bergman will be a constant reference point). In *Love and Death*, the tortured self-analysis, the absence of God, the mystic visions, dreams and nightmares are all aspects of Bergman's influence and world, though here comically inflected. More specifically, a striking composition of two faces of women – Sonia and her cousin (Jessica Harper) – as they philosophise about life, borrows from Bergman's *Persona* (1966), just as the allegorical figure of Death who plays with Woody's hero in *Love and Death* is a direct reference to Bergman's film *The Seventh Seal* (1957).

These literary and cinematic references that send up the Russian soul and make light of God's silence are entertaining but they also have serious undertones. The film debates the morality of political assassination and concludes that, if God is certainly not evil, then He is basically an underachiever. 'To love is to suffer,' says Sonia at one stage. The comic context puts the statement in inverted commas, as it were, yet one feels that really this sentiment is quite genuine and a sincere insight into the basic pathos of Woody Allen's world. Cinematically too, although the movie tosses off its influences with gay abandon, it is a work that is often visually stunning: the rolling clouds that accompany the opening narration; the majestic long shots of the battlefield; the spectacular scene at the opera. Ghislain Cloquet's photography makes this a splendid film to watch.

Love and Death displays the range of Allen's ability as well as some difficulties of technique he has not yet mastered. The opening dialogue between Boris and Sonia has some witty exchanges (Boris's comparison of Nature to an 'enormous restaurant', his

Above: In their country retreat in *Love and Death*, Sonia (Diane Keaton) and Boris savor a meal made out of snow.

examples of the kind of miracle that might convince him of God's existence – a burning bush, parting of the seas, Uncle Sasha picking up a cheque); but the close-ups are a bit bunched and the timing slightly awry, as if Allen is still not certain whether to play to the character or to the audience, or how to make the montage of his films rhythmically the same as his comedy timing. The period incongruities – his father's literal 'little bit of land', a

militant black as Boris's Russian commanding officer, Sonia's meals made out of snow, a Napoleonic aide being called Sidney Appelbaum – are inventive and sprightly. There are some fine set pieces: the mimed seduction scene between Boris and Countess Alexandrovna (Olga Georges-Picot) at the opera, all coy looks and waves behind black fans before Boris starts panting, uncontrollably; the duel, which Boris has tried to side-step by

cynical rather than purely comic debate about the absence of divine justice. But the differences are now becoming more marked: the Brooks film has no real equivalent to the intense romanticism of *Love and Death* nor its wide-ranging artistic allusions.

Woody is still the endearing incompetent, the reluctant revolutionary, but *Love and Death* shows the artistic context becoming more ambitious. Also, Woody is growing so popular as everyone's favorite failure that he is in danger of becoming a success, something that will eventually involve a radical shift in his comic persona. *Love and Death* has something of the zany quality of the early films, but its avoidance of triviality shows Allen about to become the darling of the bourgeois intellectual (something that never happened to another prodigiously gifted screen clown whom Allen much admires, Jerry Lewis). It confirms the establishment of Diane Keaton as his leading lady, with verbal timing and facial expressiveness almost as good as his own (watch the way she selects her herring merchant husband at the party, or her 'innocent' behavior at his death-bed). *Love and Death* demonstrates his increasing skill with actors: from now on, Allen's films will have strong supporting roles and will no longer be one-man shows. It shows off his growing technical ability as he moves toward becoming one of the most formally adventurous directors in modern cinema. For all these reasons, *Love and Death* remains one of Woody Allen's most fascinating films, as well as one of his funniest and one of his finest.

Below: The duel in *Love and Death*, in which Boris earns the undying respect of his opponent (Harold Gould, right) by firing into the air. The bullet hits Boris.

fast, surreal linguistic footwork worthy of Groucho Marx ('my seconds are out this morning – see my thirds . . .').

At the time it was quite common to compare *Love and Death* with Mel Brooks's similar comic venture into the world of the Russian classic *The Twelve Chairs* (1970). There are definite similarities; an unexpected visual expansiveness inspired by Eastern European locations; heroes betrayed by fate; and a

CHAPTER TWO

ART
AND
LIFE

1976-1981

Page 42: Woody Allen and Diane Keaton in *Annie Hall.*

In 1976, as a brief respite from the arduousness of writing and directing, Woody Allen agreed to take the leading role in *The Front*, a movie directed by Martin Ritt from a screenplay by Walter Bernstein. Allen accepted the part because he felt strongly about the film's theme – an attack on the blacklisting of showbusiness personalities for allegedly left-wing sympathies during the McCarthy era in the 1950s. Ritt and Bernstein had themselves been blacklisted, as had Zero Mostel who takes a leading role as a victimized comic whose despairing suicide eventually pushes Woody Allen's hero from complacency to rebellion. Mostel's appearance before the House of Un-American Activities Committee during its televised hearings was one of the few amusing episodes in that grim period (Mostel referring to his contracted employer as 'Eighteenth Century Fox' and sardonically thanking the HUAC 'for making it possible for me to be on television – I've been blacklisted from it for five years').

Below: Woody Allen appears as Howard Prince in Martin Ritt's drama about TV blacklisting, *The Front.*

Woody Allen plays Howard Prince, a cashier and small-time bookmaker who is approached by an old friend Alfred Miller (Michael Murphy) to put his name to some scripts Miller has written for a TV network. Miller himself has been blacklisted but, in return for the use of Prince's name, he will give him ten percent commission per script. Soon Prince has more clients; is fêted by the network and becomes romantically involved with its story editor, Florence Barrett (Andrea Markovicci); and finds himself acquiring and indeed basking in a reputation which is erroneous.

Things start to go comically wrong when he is asked to do rewrites at short notice (a desperate phone-call to Miller saves the day) and people begin to wonder about his supernaturally prolific output. Then things begin to go tragically wrong when the host of the series, Hecky Brown (Mostel) is himself blacklisted but offered the opportunity of reinstatement for spying on Howard Prince.

Left: Zero Mostel (seated, center) plays the tragic comedian Hecky Brown in *The Front.*

Below: Howard Prince is arrested in a scene from *The Front.*

Successive humiliations drive Hecky to suicide. Hecky's fate and Howard's growing dissatisfaction with his 'double' role combine to drive Howard inexorably toward a confrontation with the HUAC.

In retrospect, *The Front* seems a fascinating and far from marginal interlude in Woody Allen's writing and directing career. It has many ingredients of Woody Allen's own movies, particularly the films he is to make in the future. The McCarthy era in America was no laughing matter, but its frequent absurdities are finely exploited here. Some of the humor of the situation is worthy of Woody Allen's own writing: Howard's having to start borrowing great literature from the library in order to appreciate what he is credited with writing; his solemn counselling of the writers that the scripts they are asking him to front are not up to his usual standard. When compelled to face the HUAC, Howard adopts a Woody Allen-type ploy in attempting to demoralize and defeat the Committee through pedantic verbal wizardry (when asked if he knows Alfred Miller, for example, Howard replies: 'Which Alfred Miller are you referring to – and when you say "know," do you mean it in the Biblical sense or what?') Howard Prince becomes an accidental celebrity, with initial benefits and later drawbacks: the same will happen to Leonard Zelig. *The Front* opens and closes with newsreel shots of the period, accompanied over the soundtrack by Frank Sinatra's singing of 'Young at Heart.' This mock-nostalgic and ironic use of newsreel and popular music is also a part of Allen's own filmic strategy in *Take the Money and Run* and *Zelig.* Michael Murphy, who plays Allen's

best friend in *The Front*, will again play his best friend in a later film, *Manhattan*.

In *Stardust Memories*, the Woody Allen hero defines his political attitudes as follows: 'I believe in democracy, total democracy – I also believe the American system can work.' It is probably not in Woody Allen's nature to make an overtly political film himself – in *Annie Hall*, he will describe politicians' ethics as 'a notch underneath child molester' – and *The Front* is probably as far as he will go in this direction, his nearest equivalent to Chaplin's savage satire on McCarthyism, *A King in New York* (1957). It remains to be said that, although Mostel's towering performance is the most abiding memory one takes from *The Front* (and also the enormous cinematic promise, so far unfulfilled, of Andrea Marko-vicci), Woody Allen's performance is re-strained, skillful, and enormously sympathetic. At the time, with the general critical concep-tion of Allen as a brilliant gag-man, it looked a bit of an aberration. Now it looks like a portent of the deepening seriousness and artistic ambition of his future work.

It seems as if the Woody Allen film critics had all been waiting for materialized in the form of *Annie Hall* (1977), which turned out to be *the* screen romance of the late 1970s. For Woody Allen, it marked a significant shift of direction, in subject (from cine-pastiche to self-revelation) and in persona (from stooge

Right: Bedroom conversation about books, sex and cannabis: Woody Allen and Diane Keaton in *Annie Hall*.

Below: Annie Hall (Diane Keaton, left) chats to Alvy Singer (Woody Allen, right) in a New York street after their first meeting at a tennis club in *Annie Hall*.

to sage). The film's huge popularity and Oscar-winning success (Woody winning Oscars for writing and direction, Diane Keaton for best actress, the movie being voted best film) testified to his remarkable dexterity in being able to transform private angst into public art.

The strategy behind the film was probably suggested by Ingmar Bergman's *Scenes from a Marriage* (1973): rather than fit the actors to the parts, why not make a film in which you fit the parts to the actors? In *Annie Hall*, Woody Allen and Diane Keaton are both stars and part-subjects of this story of a love affair between a neurotic romantic and nervous wreck. Allen plays Alvy Singer, a stand-up comic like himself. Diane Keaton plays the title role and her family name in the film just happens to be Hall.

The autobiographical nature of the film gives it two ostensible advantages over its predecessors: realism and structure. In the past, the fantastic elements of *Sleeper* or *Everything You Always Wanted to Know About Sex* cohered uneasily with the director's personal preoccupations and anxieties, creat-ing an incongruity between form and content. In *Annie Hall*, Woody Allen solves the problems by using the camera not to tell a story but to write an essay that is part auto-biography, part personal philosophy. The form allows him to range freely over his life, surveying his schooldays ('Those who can't do, teach; those who can't teach, teach gym'), his two failed marriages and, most funda-mentally, his relationship with Annie Hall/ Diane Keaton. As well as being a survey of an age from Eisenhower ennui through Kennedy trauma to Nixonian deviousness, this struc-ture also permits Allen to insert personal preoccupations of his own – from his prefer-ence for New York over Los Angeles to his hatred of canned laughter on TV shows – without such insertions damaging the narra-tive flow of the film. In a sense, Alvy Singer *is* the narrative.

Adding greatly to the fun is the free-wheeling style of the film, which admirably

Left: Diane Keaton (left), Woody Allen (center) and Tony Roberts (right) in a scene from *Annie Hall*, with Roberts playing a familiar role as Woody's best friend.

Below: Diane Keaton and Woody Allen in *Annie Hall*, his Oscar-winning, semi-autobiographical, nervously romantic comedy.

matches its seemingly spontaneous structure of following each reminiscence as it happens. Subtitles are used for thought in Alvy and Annie's first conversation, to suggest the deaf acceleration of desire that is going on underneath their civilized discourse. The screen is sometimes split into different time-spaces in the manner of Elia Kazan's *The Arrangement* (1969), as an adult Alvy makes an appearance in his own schooldays and the scene of Annie's first date is watched and commented on by Alvy and Annie. Split screen is used, first to contrast their two families (in a subjective shot representing the point of view of Annie's anti-Semitic grandmother, Alvy will appear as a rabbi), and, secondly, to contrast their two analysts. People are interviewed on the street by the hero, who wishes to solicit advice for his emotional problems (an elderly woman can only counsel him: 'That's how people are. Love fades!') Caught in a cinema line behind a loud-mouth who insists on audibly expostulating his views about Fellini and Marshall McLuhan, Alvy can actually produce McLuhan from the cinema lobby so as to tell this man that he is talking rubbish. 'Boy', says Alvy, turning to the camera, 'if only life were like this!'

What is life like for a hero like Alvy Singer, or Woody Allen? The comic monologue which opens the film contains two jokes which contain the truths about existence, according to him. The first concerns two old ladies in a holiday resort: one complains that the food is 'really terrible' and the other agrees, adding 'and such small portions.' This is a basic tenet of the Singer/Allen philosophy: life is terrible, but you must live it to the full, suicide being no solution (as the Woody Allen character in *Hannah and Her Sisters* will find). The second basic joke is the Groucho Marx gag about refusing to join any club which would accept him as a member. The reluctance to accept membership of the human race, yet the longing for assimilation is a fundamental dichotomy of the Woody Allen persona.

Right: Alvy talks to Annie (Diane Keaton) in a still from *Annie Hall*, which was used to advertise the film.

Below: Alvy apprehensively prepares to boil a lobster in *Annie Hall*.

How does such a philosophy cope with human relationships? Scenes of the romance with Annie Hall are spiced with domestic wit, Alvy unable to boil lobster, Annie unable to deal with a spider in the bathroom, and the relationship finally compared by Alvy to a 'dead shark', dying because it is not moving forward. Annie is intimidated by Alvy's intellectual superiority and condescension; Alvy is a little envious and disorientated by Annie's success as a singer. He would not belong in the Californian environment which becomes increasingly her milieu. Woody Allen crystallizes Alvy's unfitness for LA's laid-back lifestyle in a single image: attempting to behave cool and inhale cocaine, Alvy only succeeds in sneezing out the cocaine all over the sofa.

'Hardly my *8½*,' said Woody Allen about *Annie Hall*, 'more like my *2½*.' He has intimated that he felt the film was rather overrated and that he himself felt more affection at this time for *Love and Death*. Diane Keaton's performance is brilliantly skillful and expertly developed (compare her awkward early rendering of 'It Had to Be You' to her later superbly professional account of the song, 'Seems like Old Times' to suggest Annie's development as an entertainer). Yet, behind Annie Hall's walking ragbag of endearing confusion, one rather misses the actress who gave us the personification of stable, fresh feminity in *Play It Again, Sam*. It is not simply a change of part, it is as if the acting mechanism has become more mannered. Also the shift in Woody Allen's persona from being an embodiment of urban anxiety to being an authority on it is not without its suspicions of smug superiority. It is a deft comedy, unusually outspoken in its airing of sexual problems and with a remarkable array of supporting performers in small roles, including Christopher Walken, Shelley Duvall, Beverley D'Angelo and Sigourney Weaver.

Although it ultimately seems an altogether smaller film than *Love and Death*, lacking its intellectual and comic range and resonance, it was probably praised so highly at the time because it fitted so snugly the prototype Woody Allen film which the critics had so insistently clamored for. However, his next film to be released, *Interiors*, was a different matter altogether.

Top: A meeting with Annie's family, Grammy Hall (Helen Ludlam, left) and Mom Hall (Colleen Dewhurst, bottom right).

Above: Alvy, Rob (Tony Roberts, center) and Annie (Diane Keaton, right) in *Annie Hall*.

Top: Richard Jordan and Diane Keaton play an artistic wife and husband in *Interiors,* Woody Allen's first straight drama.

Above: Mary Beth Hurt as the unfulfilled Joey in *Interiors.*

With a perversity that was to become characteristic during this phase of his development, Woody Allen followed his most acclaimed film with one of his most openly contentious and controversial. *Interiors* (1978) is intense chamber-drama, a study of family breakdown that makes his world suddenly seem less Chaplinesque than Chekhovian. Three sisters are disorientated when their father leaves home for a 'trial separation' from his wife and then re-marries. The mother has a breakdown and will later commit suicide. Allen does not appear but directs with an austerity that brings the American movie closer to European art film than at almost any time in its history. *Interiors* inevitably drew comparisons with Bergman, whose similar themes of love, death and art are now starkly on the surface of Allen's movie.

Although respectfully reviewed in some quarters, *Interiors* seemed to many American critics a perverse denial by Allen of his unique comic gifts in favor of humorless pretentiousness. In Europe, the response to the film was generally more positive. This was not a betrayal of talent but a burgeoning, rather in the manner of Chaplin's *A Woman of Paris* (1923) when he suddenly decided to make a serious and searing study of emotional frailty. *Interiors* is particularly impressive in its precise visual design. Rooms become reflections of lives that are disciplined but rigid, decorous but lacking all vitality. Color becomes expressive of emotional states. When their father introduces his lady-friend Pearl (Maureen Stapleton) into the household, her bright red dress blazes new life against the family's middle-class grayness and serves as a red rag in particular to the youngest daughter Joey, played by Mary Beth Hurt, who regards Pearl as a 'vulgarian.'

One of the most likeable things about the film is its generosity of sympathy. The father could have been cast as the villain, but so perfectly is the part written and played (E G Marshall giving the finest performance in his long film career) that the pain of his separation is keenly felt. Appreciative of the home his wife Eve (Geraldine Page) has provided and grateful for her support, he has only slowly come to realize that this harmony had blocked the flow of real feelings. 'It was like an ice palace ... Then suddenly, one day ... an enormous abyss opened up beneath out feet. And I was staring into a face I didn't recognize.' Ostensibly the contrast between the bold radiance of Pearl and the pale neurosis of Eve might seem a little unbalanced. Yet Pearl's vitality masks a certain insecurity and lack of poise (she seems distraught when she clumsily smashes a vase at her wedding reception), and Eve's ugly despair conveys a nevertheless poignant sense of an ordered life thrown into chaos and unable to recapture a sense of equilibrium. There are not many movies that spend so much care in analyzing the emotional lives of the older generation. *Interiors* does this with great sensitivity.

The three sisters are also struggling for personal fulfillment, with varying degrees of success, Flyn (Kristin Griffith) seems the

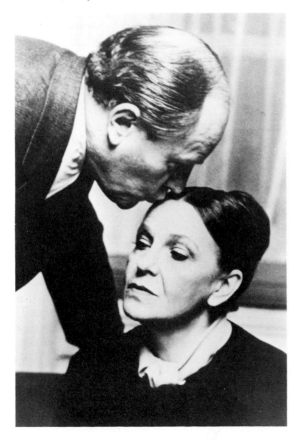

most superficial of them – an actress on television – yet she has a spontaneity and a self-detachment that is refreshingly different from her two sisters. Renata's husband, Frederick (Richard Jordan) condescendingly describes Flyn as 'form without content' (he will later attempt to rape her, after smugly telling her: 'It's been such a long time since I made love to a woman that I didn't feel inferior to'). In fact, Frederick's slick remark will rebound against himself and the others, for it is they, not Flyn, who, in contrast to the decorous externals of their lives, are floundering within. Joey has all the anguish of the artistic temperament without, alas, any of the talent. Renata (Diane Keaton) has the poetic gift, but is suffering from a crisis of self-confidence. She seems a kind of Virginia Woolf heroine, with a room of her own and immense writing ability, but with an obsession with death and an overwhelming sense of panic and fear of the outside world. ('The door opens, and the tiger leaps,' is the way Ms Woolf described such panic in *The Waves*. It would have been a good alternative title for the movie, with its beach house setting and its

Above: Renata (Diane Keaton, left) and Flyn (Kristin Griffith, right) talk while strolling along the beach in *Interiors*.

Left: E G Marshall and Geraldine Page as the estranged husband and wife in *Interiors*.

A JACK ROLLINS-CHARLES H. JOFFE PRODUCTION

"INTERIORS"_{AA}

KRISTIN GRIFFITH
MARY BETH HURT
RICHARD JORDAN
DIANE KEATON
E.G. MARSHALL
GERALDINE PAGE
MAUREEN STAPLETON
SAM WATERSTON
Director of Photography GORDON WILLIS
Executive Producer ROBERT GREENHUT
Produced by CHARLES H. JOFFE

Written and Directed by WOODY ALLEN

United Artists
A Transamerica Company

Above: The poster for *Interiors*, featuring the three sisters and emphasizing the Chekhovian atmosphere. The advertising for Woody Allen's films will become increasingly spare and restrained.

Right: Kristin Griffith plays Flyn, the least intense and self-absorbed of the sisters in *Interiors*.

emotional storms which will submerge one character and almost destroy another). Each of these characters is sharply etched and beautifully acted. As *Hannah and Her Sisters* will also reveal, Allen is a remarkably astute observer of the subtle jealousies which develop within families.

Interiors certainly proclaims Woody Allen's ambitions as a serious artist, but one should not imply that the film is devoid of light, humor or irony. Often one senses a delicate satire on artistic people who live their lives too intensely, particularly in an arty conversation over the dinner table about a recent evening in the theater, in which ethical niceties about the play's characterization are swiftly punctured by Pearl ('One guy was a squealer, the other guy wasn't. I liked the guy that wasn't . . . Did I miss something?') How well this scene is written, edited and directed – the gathering tension as the daughters instinctively begin to goad Pearl, the men relax in detached amusement, and each character's position and opinion about Pearl is discreetly established, through how each looks and what he or she does, or does not, say. Almost equally good is the scene around the breakfast table when the father announces his decision to leave, and in which the tone of civilized reasonableness cannot quite disguise the sound of a bombshell exploding irrevocably beneath these people's lives – like Pearl's smashing of their mother's vase.

At the time, *Interiors* seemed an advance for Woody Allen in three particular areas – in the solidity of the characterization, the excellence of the ensemble performances, and in the objective refinement of its handling of the themes of art and alienation. It looks no less impressive today, particularly in comparison with Robert Redford's Oscar-winning *Ordinary People* (1980), which is thematically similar (also about a drowning, mental collapse, decaying marriage and with a traumatized wife with an obsession about order), but looks so much more glossy, superficial and, well, ordinary. *Interiors* is about exceptional people; it is an exceptional film. It is cool, contemplative, intricately structured, a flawless miniature, with a pale beauty of its own, resembling that of the white roses with which the three sisters honor the memory of their dead mother.

'"Chapter One. He adored New York City. He idolized it out of all proportion." Uh, no, make that: "He romanticized it out of all proportion . . ."' With this opening narration, set to a series of shots of the New York skyline and accompanied over the soundtrack by Gershwin's 'Rhapsody in Blue', the critics could be assured instantly that Woody Allen

Top: Joey (Mary Beth Hurt, left) and Renata (Diane Keaton, right) prepare to have another argument about what is best for their mother in *Interiors.*

Above: Woody Allen directs Diane Keaton as Renata in *Interiors.*

Left: Renata (Diane Keaton), and Frederick (Richard Jordan) prepare themselves for the wedding of Renata's father in *Interiors.* Their poses suggest the growing friction and distance developing in their marriage.

Right: Renata (Diane Keaton) on the Bergmanesque beach in *Interiors.*

Below: Mary (Diane Keaton) and Isaac at the Whitney Museum in *Manhattan.*

was back stalking his familiar territory. *Manhattan* (1979) is more fictionalized than *Annie Hall*, but the milieu is similar, and it elaborates on similar themes. Allen himself described the theme of the film as 'the problem of trying to live a decent life amidst all the junk of contemporary culture – the temptations, the seductions.'

One example of that junk for Isaac Davis (Woody Allen) is the novelization of screenplays, something undertaken by a Philadelphia intellectual, Mary Wilke (Diane Keaton) in *Manhattan*, who yet still has the arrogance to proclaim an Academy of the Overrated and nominate for inclusion such giants as Scott Fitzgerald, Gustav Mahler, Heinrich Böll and, most outrageously, Ingmar Bergman. As Woody Allen's character, Isaac Davis remarks: 'If she had made one more remark about Bergman, I would've knocked her other contact lens out.' Another example of cultural junk is the publication of the most intimate details of people's personal lives, irrespective of the suffering it might cause to one or other of the personalities involved. This is another of Isaac Davis's problems, for his ex-wife (Meryl Streep) has written a book about their disastrous marriage, which is not only a best-seller but which might well be filmed. Isaac himself concedes that he is a contributor to cultural junk, writing material for television which his bosses think is great and he believes is totally empty: 'You know, these guys sit in front of their sets and the gamma rays eat the white cells of their brains out.' He is trying to write a novel while his best friend Yale (Michael Murphy) is slaving away at a biography of Eugene O'Neill. In both cases, the chaos of their emotional lives makes it likely that neither book will be completed.

Isaac is involved in a passionate romance with a girl, Tracy (Mariel Hemingway) so much younger than himself that he has to keep checking that his references to people like Rita Hayworth and Veronica Lake are not going over her head. His best friend, Yale, is having an affair with Mary Wilke, whom Isaac first loathes and then comes to love. Isaac moves in with Mary when Yale returns to his wife, but this leaves Tracy heartbroken. But when Yale and Mary resume their relationship, Isaac has belatedly to recognize that he has cast aside a girl whom he truly valued. His final scene with Tracy is a reversal of their previous times together, with Isaac now seeming awkward and hesitant and Tracy seeming serene, self-assured and mature. 'You have to have a little faith in people,' she tells Isaac: his reaction shot at that is a final close-up encapsulating acceptance, sorrow and goodbye, clearly modelled on Chaplin's

Above: 'It's such a beautiful Sunday,' Mary has said, but this is what happens on her day out at Central Park with Isaac in *Manhattan*.

Left: Isaac discusses his friend's new girlfriend with his own girlfriend, Tracy (Mariel Hemingway) in *Manhattan*.

Top: Romantic deflation in *Manhattan:* taking Mary (Diane Keaton) on a rowboat on Central Park lake, Isaac runs his hand in the water – his hand gets covered in dirt.

Above: Isaac summarizes the main themes of *Manhattan.*

famous last shot in *City Lights* (1931).

For all the offbeat humor (like that splendid moment of romantic deflation when, on a boat in Central Park with Mary, Isaac runs his hand lightly in the water and finds it entirely covered with mud and dirt), *Manhattan* is designed as a reflective, serious picture. Gordon Willis's black-and-white photography is a hymn to New York, fashioning magical images from Isaac and Mary's nocturnal

conversation in Central Park and their whispered exchanges in silhouette in the aquarium. And after what they saw as the baleful bellyaching of *Interiors*, the critics were entranced by this study of the emotional alienation of the Manhattan intelligentsia, which came gift-wrapped by Allen in the most beguiling combination of wit and nostalgia. The critic Andrew Sarris described the film as 'the only truly great American movie of the Seventies.' Ironically, Sarris had previously disputed Woody Allen's qualifications for being a convincing lover in the cinema. Allen's casting of the chubby, balding, Wallace Shawn as Mary's irresistibly sexy ex-husband in *Manhattan* serves as a kind of riposte to this: 'It's amazing how subjective all that stuff is,' says Isaac.

However, the critics who had doubts about the self-centeredness of *Annie Hall* were even more dismayed by *Manhattan*, though they were admittedly in a small minority. There is something about Isaac's name-dropping – 'When it comes to relationships with women, I'm the winner of the August Strindberg Award' – that smacks a little of cultural snobbery. When Isaac nobly quits his humiliating job, cutely entertains his son, protests against pollution and neo-Nazism, one has the uncomfortable sense of special pleading on behalf of the character. This is reinforced by the fact that he is given all the jokes. 'You look so beautiful I can hardly keep my eyes on the meter,' he says to Mary when they are sharing a taxi. 'You think you're God!' cries Yale at him, to which Isaac replies: 'I gotta model myself after someone!' The humor is fine but so set up that realism is undermined. Mary and Yale are suddenly less like characters than straight men feeding cues to the main comic star. Even the timing is slightly awry. In the afore-mentioned exchange with Yale in a classroom, the camera rests on a skeleton skull for such an unconscionable length of time that when Isaac starts to address it as if he were Hamlet with Yorick's skull ('Someday we're gonna look like him . . . he was probably one of the beautiful people'), the effect seems predictable, contrived and no longer funny. This is a film in which accusations of narcissism directed at the leading actor would be hard to deny, and the comic selfishness which is at the heart of the film undermines the urgency of its theme.

If *Manhattan* soothed most of Woody Allen's admirers after the culture shock of *Interiors*, his following film, *Stardust Memories* (1980) again embroiled him in controversy. *Annie Hall* was an autobiographical essay, written by the camera; *Stardust Memories* is a critical essay in celluloid, a

resumé and assessment of Allen's own career and his screen persona. The central situation is that a comedy director, Sandy Bates – to all intents and purposes, Woody Allen himself – who wants to make serious films and who, at a stage in his life where both personal and creative channels seem to be blocked, reminisces about and criticizes his past achievements and relationships. The focus of the action is a festival of the director's own films. Some defense is offered against those detractors who dismiss Woody Allen's films as narcissistic ('If I did identify with a God,' says Sandy, 'it wouldn't be Narcissus, it would be Zeus'). Yet *Stardust Memories* is an act of self-criticism more than self-love, a state of mind intensified by what Bates, in his particular harassed and paranoid vision, sees as the indiscriminate and ill-informed acclaim of many of his fans and critics.

It is not unique for an artist to lash out at his followers – one thinks of Pope's brilliant satirical poem, 'Epistle to Doctor Arbuthnot,' in which he routs all sycophants – but he runs the risk of offending and antagonizing friends as well. Many American critics were quite appalled by Allen's attitudes in *Stardust Memories*: Pauline Kael referred to the film as a 'horrible betrayal' while Richard Roud dubbed it an 'unmitigated failure'. Why must

Below: Isaac (Woody Allen) confronts his ex-wife Jill (Meryl Streep), who has just published a book about their marriage, in *Manhattan*.

Woody Allen
Charlotte Rampling
Jessica Harper
Marie-Christine Barrault
Tony Roberts

Stardust Memories
AA

A Jack Rollins - Charles H. Joffe *Production* "Stardust Memories"
Producer Robert Greenhut *Written and Directed by* Woody Allen *Executive Producers* Jack Rollins - Charles H. Joffe
Director of Photography Gordon Willis *Production Designer* Mel Bourne
🆃 United Artists A Transamerica Company

Above: Poster for *Stardust Memories,* one of Woody Allen's most controversial movies.

he embark on this act of character assassination, even to the point in the film of having himself shot? Why cannot he be content with making people laugh, as in his 'early *funny* films'? In Europe, where the critics in general were less infatuated by his comic gifts but more intrigued by his artistic ambitions, *Stardust Memories* was more thoughtfully received as a bold and brave creation in which the creator takes stock of the split between reputation and self-assessment, between what he values in art and what the public seem to want.

In bravely confronting the failure of success for a man who wants to be taken seriously as an artist, *Stardust Memories* has the brilliant idea of rendering the American Dream in the visual style of European alienation. It is as if Preston Sturges's *Sullivan's Travels* (1941), which also has a film-within-a-film structure and a comedy director who wants to make a serious social statement, has collided head-on with Fellini's *8½* (1963), which is about a director with a creative block who has to ransack his

memories for inspiration and consolation. It also has echoes of Bergman's *Persona,* with its sense of personal breakdown and the way art scavenges life for material, and of Henry King's *The Gunfighter* (1950), in its observations of a man whose fame prevents him from leading a normal life and leaves him vulnerable to threats of violence incited by envy. As Chaplin did with his character of Monsieur Verdoux, Allen has taken a lovable comedy persona to an extreme where suddenly the victim cannot forbear striking back.

Clearly the superstar director-hero of *Stardust Memories* is a long way from the fumbling film critic of *Play It Again, Sam*; indeed, *he* could be telling Humphrey Bogart what to do. The movie dares to antagonize its audience by presenting a hero generally contemptuous of his fans, more obviously flawed, abrasive and pressurized than Allen's usual hero, and whose self-absorption is submitted to a more critical judgment. Whereas *Manhattan* implicitly applauded its hero's sympathetic liberalism, *Stardust Memories*

58

questions much more openly the moral stance of the bourgeois intellectual whose sensitivity to injustice and human suffering is often matched only by his inability or disinclination to alleviate any of it. The film cannot offer any solutions, but the questions are more honestly and agonizingly posed, and less smoothly elided by complacent self-mockery. What haunts the hero of *Stardust Memories* is not the issue of talent but that of courage and commitment. A huge picture of a doomed, tormented youth in Hanoi dominates his wall, and in Allen's words, his 'metaphor for life is a concentration camp.' Nothing is more startling and shocking than his comment to an old schoolfriend about his luck: 'If I was not born in Brooklyn, if I had been born in Poland, or Berlin, I'd be a lampshade today, right?' Wit has rarely seemed closer to self-loathing.

In fact, the film tingles with a sense of despair – creative, personal, moral. The sense of breakdown is mirrored by a structure which drives sideways and upward as well as forward, and with scenes that peter out before a true climax is reached. Solitary

Left: Woody Allen plays tormented film director, Sandy Bates in *Stardust Memories.*

Below: Sandy relaxes with an old girlfriend Isobel (Marie-Christine Barrault) while her children order ice cream in *Stardust Memories.*

59

images hover between dream and nightmare – the hero pulls desperately at an emergency cord which keeps expanding indefinitely in his hands, or a man on an exercise bike reaches furtively for a cigarette, his physical fanaticism fighting a precarious battle for supremacy with his personal neurosis. The critique of a drug-ridden American culture and the emptiness of intellectual banter is caustic, for once, more than charming. On the whole, it is an extraordinarily creative use of self-doubt from a man whose personal appraisal does not square easily with that of his admirers.

The song, 'Easy to Love' is heard over the soundtrack during part of the film's haunting finale, which mixes fantasy, death, a grudging premiere and the director alone in a deserted cinema. The context gives the familiar tune an angle of irony – far removed from the unmodulated nostalgia of the soundtrack for *Manhattan* – particularly as people have been watching a film that is hard even to like. 'Easy to Love' might refer to Woody Allen's uneasy reassessment of his lovable screen persona which he feels has been accepted a little too smugly, a smugness which this film is concerned to rebuke. Above all, the melody makes one think. For if there is a consistent refrain in his films, it is that, in Woody Allen, love is never easy.

In fact, this is one of his primary themes. For all the talk of Allen's obsession with urban neurosis, and the self as career, or whatever, by this stage the theme that is emerging most insistently is the search for the Perfect Woman. The principal quality which distinguishes Woody Allen from comic forebears such as Groucho and Hope, comic contemporaries such as Mel Brooks, and even European influences like Bergman and Fellini, is an authentic romantic yearning. Indeed the film-makers he resembles most in *Stardust Memories* are the Truffaut of *Day for Night* (1973) and *The Green Room* (1978) and the Godard of *Pierrot le Fou* (1965), with similar obsessions and references: the pains of love, trust and betrayal in sexual relationships, the tension between fantasy and reality, art and life, literature and cinema. The foregrounding

Above: Sandy talks to Isobel (Marie-Christine Barrault) in *Stardust Memories*, one of the three women in the film who seem to offer a tantalizing romantic ideal.

Right: 'I don't eat rodent,' Sandy tells his cook (Dorothy Leon), who has just set fire to his cooker in *Stardust Memories*.

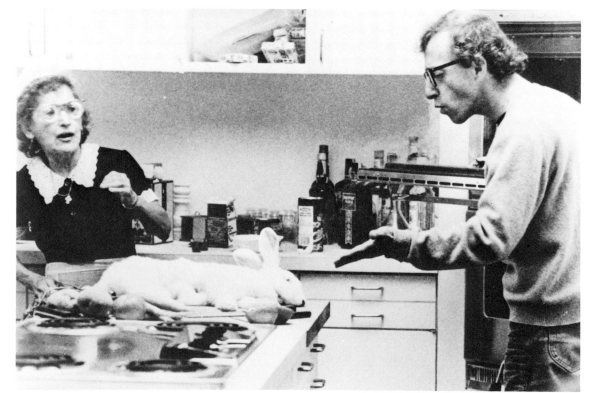

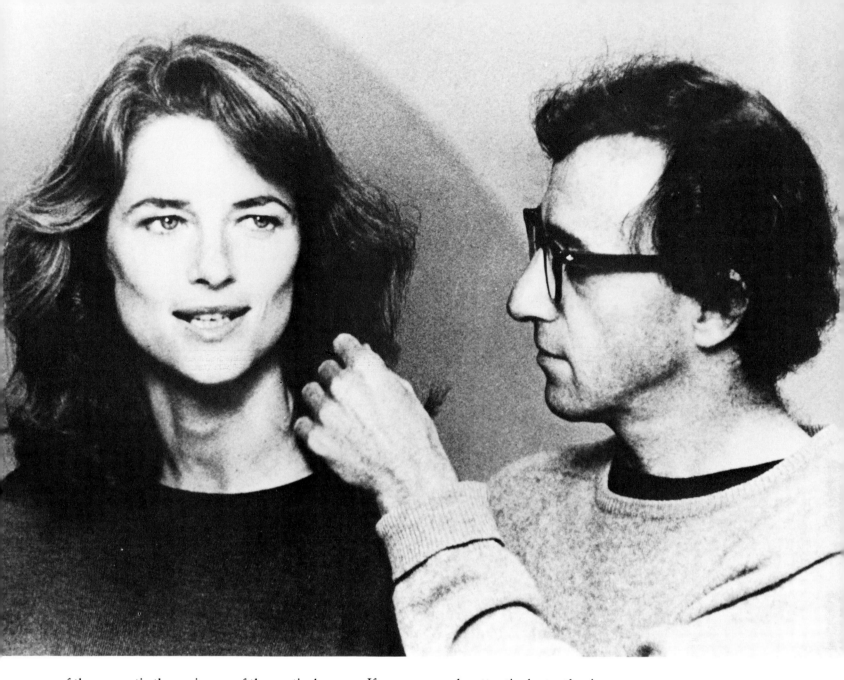

of the romantic theme is one of the particular distinctions of *Stardust Memories*, and the actresses in the film – Charlotte Rampling, Marie-Christine Barrault and Jessica Harper – are directed with particular sympathy and imagination, being presences seen and felt as if in a fevered dream. One of the main triggers of Allen's artistic imagination, as for Truffaut, has been the mystique of feminity. Amid the truculent tone, the profoundly disturbing self-analysis, the odd allusions to flight (the artist as conjurer or arrogant Icarus?) and the even odder interrogation of the hero by outer space aliens (what price Woody Allen's cinema and civilization in an industry and a country given over to Star Wars?), there is one moment of beauty and repose, and it is the moment that gives the film its title. The hero remembers one afternoon in which he listened to Louis Armstrong singing Hoagy Carmichael's 'Stardust' and simultaneously looking across at his beautiful girlfriend, Dorrie (Charlotte Rampling), the hero grasps the harmony and the happiness that he has sought.

If one responds attentively to the inner music of *Stardust Memories*, the work one will hear is Mahler's marvelous Tenth Symphony. (Mahler, one might recall, is one of the inclusions in Mary Wilke's Academy of the Overrated in *Manhattan* which so enrages Isaac). Like the Mahler work, *Stardust Memories* is fragmented, death-ridden, precariously balanced between self-obsessed sentimentality and a universal poignancy. Also like the Mahler, its broken-backed romanticism is contaminated by the anguish of the age, a tension that threatens to explode the work from within into chaos. Yet, the final ten minutes of both works achieve a momentary mood of purest radiance and sublime serenity that is profoundly moving. *Stardust Memories* is one of those purgatorial artistic journeys that can make or break its creator, and significantly, it seemed to represent the culmination for Allen of his cinema of self-revelation. But its bold brilliance still resounds, and, if any film of his deserves the label 'masterpiece', this is it.

Above: Woody Allen and Charlotte Rampling as film director and star in *Stardust Memories.*

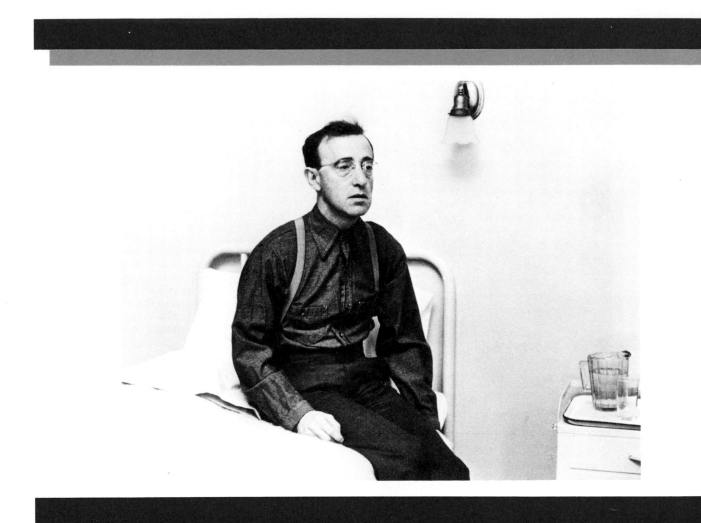

CHAPTER THREE

PUTTING ON THE STYLE

1982-

After the autobiography and rigorous self-analysis of such movies as *Annie Hall* and *Stardust Memories*, it was perhaps inevitable that Woody Allen would step back and make a more objective contemplation of his art. His next four films were to initiate a third phase in his development in which the screen persona of Woody Allen, as developed in movies from *Love and Death* to *Manhattan*, recedes more into the background and one senses his presence more forcefully behind the camera than in front. All four movies are rather withdrawn miniatures, all less than an hour and a half in length, and only one and a half of them in color. All of them have their serious side, but are not nearly so bleakly intense as *Interiors* or *Stardust Memories*. All are quite funny, but not nearly so uproarious as *Take the Money and Run* and *Bananas*; all are quite personal, but less self-absorbed than *Annie Hall* and less self-lacerating than *Stardust Memories*. As a final but significant footnote, they are movies which indicate the displacement of Diane Keaton as Woody's romantic ideal in favor of Mia Farrow.

The four films are looser, more experimental, and, in some way, they are as interesting technically as they are thematically. Who would have imagined that Woody would move from the jazzy rhythms of *Sleeper* to the Mendelssohnian airiness of *A Midsummer Night's Sex Comedy* (1982)? Who could have guessed that the director of so cinematically raw a film as *Bananas* would, in ten years'

time, be capable of a technical tour-de-force like *Zelig?* Who could have suspected that the maker of *Everything You Always Wanted to Know About Sex* would occasionally move so decisively to the art end of American cinema and, in films like *Interiors* and *Zelig*, produce work as hermetic and personal as the more oddball efforts of Robert Altman or Francis Coppola? The question is: is it progression, or regression? Is he developing into genuine artistry or retreating into pretentious esotericism? This was the main critical argument over this quartet of films. To put it more bluntly, were they gems, or fakes?

The only dud seems to me to be *A Midsummer Night's Sex Comedy*, a period pastoral of promiscuity that seems as ungainly as its title. Two couples spend the weekend at the home of a Wall Street broker and amateur inventor, Andrew (Woody Allen) and his wife, Adrian (Mary Steenburgen), who are having marital problems. The guests are a hedonist doctor, Maxwell (Tony Roberts) and his willing nurse companion, Dulcy (Julie Hagerty); and a pompous philosophy professor Leopold (José Ferrer), who is Adrian's cousin and Leopold's bride-to-be, Ariel (Mia Farrow), with whom Andrew was once infatuated. The weekend develops into a series of changing partners and secret assignations, an emotional intoxication that is clearly stimulated by the clear country air.

The chain of frustration is broken when Andrew's romantic infatuation with Ariel

Right: José Ferrer plays a philosophy professor and Julie Hagerty a nurse in *A Midsummer Night's Sex Comedy.*

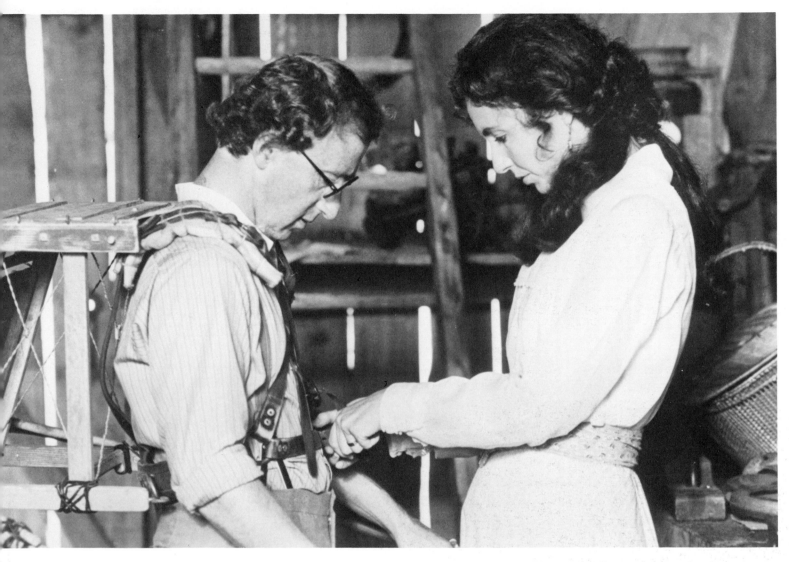

culminates in failed love-making, the frogs and crickets giving them both a headache; when Leopold satisfies his desire for Dulcy (though when she requests that he bite her harder, he has to confess that these are not his teeth); and when Maxwell, who is now in love with Ariel, confesses to Andrew that he has once slept with Adrian. Andrew and Adrian are reunited; Maxwell and Ariel come together; and Leopold dies in sexual ecstasy, entering

the spirit world with a renunciation of his materialist philosophy and declaring that 'these woods *are* enchanted.'

As the title suggests, the film borrows freely from Shakespeare's *A Midsummer Night's Dream* (enchanted woods and exchanges of lovers) and uses Mendelssohn's incidental music to accompany some of the action (the scherzo for the agitated assignations, the intermezzo for the midnight meetings that misfire). Mendelssohn's Scotch Symphony is also employed for a dazzling nature montage and the finale of the Violin Concerto for a skittish picnic: we are a long way here from the popular music and modest pretensions of Allen's earlier movies. We are also again in Bergmanland, with a plot that has many points of comparison with *Smiles of a Summer Night* (1955), notably in the jealous love of an older man for a younger girl. But the parallel that most comes to mind is probably Jean Renoir. When a jealous Leopold spies on Maxwell and Ariel through a telescope, one is reminded of a similar traumatic moment when guilty lovers are espied in the hunting scene of *La Règle du Jeu* (1939). The theme of the film – urbanites melted and mellowed by Nature –

Above: The wife (Mary Steenburgen), helps her inventor husband (Woody Allen) with his flying machine in *A Midsummer Night's Sex Comedy.*

Left: Gunnar Björnstrand (left), Eva Dahlbeck (center) and Jarl Kulle (right) in a scene from Ingmar Bergman's *Smiles of a Summer Night,* to which Woody's *Midsummer* opus pays overt homage.

is similar to Renoir's *Le Déjeuner sur l'Herbe* (1959). Indeed, the painting of that name by Jean's father, Auguste, probably inspired the whole visual style of the film, whose beautiful images (photography as usual by Gordon Willis) often recall the canvases of French Impressionism.

The tone of the film is whimsical rather than witty. One is charmed more than amused by Andrew's inventions, which include a machine for peeling fruit and vegetables and a bicycle helicopter which at one moment allows him to

Below: Maxwell (Tony Roberts) falls in love with Ariel in *A Midsummer Night's Sex Comedy.*

have a secret conversation with Ariel outside her bedroom window without his actually having to climb a ladder to her room. The professor's pomposity is amusingly punctured, partly by progressively undermining his rational certainties and partly by deflating his displays of intellect (when he loftily informs his companions that Raphael had fainted when he first saw the Sistine ceiling, Andrew mildly retorts: 'Had he eaten?') In one scene, his earnest rendering of a German *lied* is crosscut with an equally earnest whispered conversation as Maxwell tells Ariel of his feelings and tries to arrange an illicit meeting. Andrew overhears their conversation with a mixture of tact (he is politely listening to Leopold) and tension (he is jealous), but is then sexually assaulted on the kitchen table by Adrian ('we can't make love where we eat oatmeal!' he protests) while Leopold is crooning the Lord's Prayer in the adjoining room. Leopold would be an insufferable character were it not for José Ferrer's well judged performance, which might have encouraged Woody in the future to employ the talents of veteran Hollywood performers (Van Johnson appears in *The Purple Rose of Cairo*, Lloyd Nolan in *Hannah and Her Sisters*). Ferrer's is the only performance that seems to have a feeling for the turn of the century period and style. The others seem like contemporary Manhattan-ites unaccountably caught in a time warp.

At one stage, Andrew comments: 'sex

Right: The professor (José Ferrer) performs a German *lied* while the guests are crackling with sexual tension in *A Midsummer Night's Sex Comedy.* Mary Steenburgen is at the piano.

Far right, above: A day in the country in *A Midsummer Night's Sex Comedy.*

Far right, below: Andrew discusses lost romantic opportunities with Ariel (Mia Farrow) in *A Midsummer Night's Sex Comedy.*

alleviates tension and love causes it.' The tension between love and lust is a major theme in the film, as is the tension between reason and imagination. The film's conclusion is that there is magic in the air and more to life than meets the eye, even if the cerebral style and rather self-conscious rural romps are more reminiscent of Leopold's stiffness than Maxwell's emotional impulsiveness or Andrew's eccentric inventiveness. It is an awkward mixture in which the moral nuance of a Henry James has somehow got trapped in the mechanics of a French farce.

Its significance in Woody Allen's development is the appearance in it of Mia Farrow, who was to be his leading lady in his next four films, and its stylistic novelty, in which familiar Allen characters (embarrassed former lovers, best friends who become romantic rivals) are placed in an unfamiliar environment. Fey and rather literary symbolism (moonlight for romance, arrows for desire, flight equalling imagination) is given unusual emphasis. Romance triumphs over realism and mysticism over materialism, and the movie walks a tightrope between fun and frivolousness with some uncomfortable

at all but constitutes one of the most remarkable period and stylistic simulations attempted by any film-maker.

The eponymous hero of Woody Allen's *Zelig* (1983) is a human chameleon capable of emulating the appearance and speech of anybody he is with, whether that person be Black or Red Indian, a Chinaman or a Chicago gangster with a scar. When the phenomenon is investigated by a New York psychiatrist, Dr Eudora Fletcher (Mia Farrow) it turns out that Zelig can also emulate the other person's personality and speech patterns. In her presence he becomes an arrogant psychoanalyst who fell out with Freud over the subject of penis envy ('in my opinion women have it too') and who boasts of a case where he is treating two pairs of schizophrenic Siamese twins ('I receive fees from eight people'). His celebrity is assured when his sister and brother-in-law exploit his 'deformity' in the manner of the 1980 film, *The Elephant Man* (another monochrome period piece about a 'freak'). However, his fame changes to notoriety when, on the eve of his planned wedding to Eudora, a paternity suit against him is filed, which sets off a chain of legal charges against him in his infinite other identities. He disappears but Eudora spots him, in brown uniform, in a newsreel about the Nazis, and the two are re-united and escape back to America, receiving a ticker-tape welcome home.

More startling than the story of *Zelig* is the

lurches toward the latter. It is Woody Allen's most painterly film, his personal magic lantern show, but it never seems emotionally authentic. Like Woody Allen's inventor-character, it makes a brave attempt to soar into the world of enchantment, but one always feels that the director is relieved when he is back on solid ground. In the light of this, it is probably significant that the film's most memorable image is its most cynically clinical: the sustained shot of the drawing of a skeleton as the oily Maxwell proposes his dirty weekend to the willing Dulcy – an image that crystallizes his bluntly anatomical view of human personality, particularly women.

One of the features of *A Midsummer Night's Sex Comedy* is its suspicion of words, that intellectualize and rationalize and attempt to contain life's mystery through insistent explanation: here natural beauty and emotional instinct will make words evaporate and will release feelings. The word, the gag, the wise-crack become less important in Woody Allen's next three films, as he explores the cinema's ability to tell enchanted stories and to capture the surface of the visible world. His next film has no extended dialogue exchanges

way in which the film is done. Like Woody Allen's first film, *Take the Money and Run*, it is a mock-documentary and a pastiche of the bio-pic, but on an infinitely more elaborate scale. Fictional footage of *Zelig* is carefully matched with 1920s and 1930s newsreel footage of real-life luminaries like Babe Ruth, Jack Dempsey and Adolf Hitler. In a scene where he appears with Pope Pius XI at the Vatican, Allen seems to be reprising that ancient joke about the man who knew every-

Left: Zelig with his sympathetic psychiatrist, Dr Eudora Fletcher (Mia Farrow).

Below: Zelig and his psychiatrist become engaged in *Zelig*.

one ('I don't know who the man with the funny hat is, but the fellow with him is Leonard Zelig'). When he spots Eudora in the crowd at a huge Hitler rally and starts waving to her from behind the platform, we have a brilliant Chaplinesque moment where our (literally) Everyman hero upstages the Great Dictator.

The creation of such footage took three years, and its grainy authenticity is a stroke of genius from cameraman Gordon Willis. It is augmented by a brilliant score from Dick Hyman, who composes new songs ('Leonard the Lizard') and modifies old favorites ('You're the tops, you're Leonard Zelig') to evoke the period. We learn that Warner Brothers made a film about Zelig in 1935, *The Changing Man*, which would make it not only Hollywood's first anti-Nazi movie (a dig at Hollywood's slowness in committing itself against Fascism) but which is also a brilliant pastiche of thirties movie-making that anticipates the more extended cinematic joke of *The Purple Rose of Cairo*. (Another connection: Zelig arrives home to a hero's welcome, like Lindberg; the actor, Gil Shepherd, in *The Purple Rose of Cairo* will wish to play the part of Charles Lindberg on screen.)

Right: Marvel or freak? Zelig with his doctors.

Below: The poster from *Zelig*, with the multitude of different signatures suggesting the theme of the elusiveness of identity.

Zelig
Zelig
Zelig
Zelig
ZELIG
Zelig

Eine
JACK ROLLINS und CHARLES H. JOFFE Produktion

WOODY ALLEN   MIA FARROW

Schnitt   Kostume   Produktions-Design
SUSAN E. MORSE   SANTO LOQUASTO   MEL BOURNE
Kamera   Exekutiv-Produzent   Produktion
GORDON WILLIS   CHARLES H. JOFFE   ROBERT GREENHUT
Drehbuch und Regie   Ein ORION Film
WOODY ALLEN   im Verleih der Warner-Columbia. A Warner Communications Company
                    © 1983 Orion Pictures and Warner Bros. All Rights Reserved.

A further sophistication to this dazzling structure is the testimony of 'witnesses' on the phenomenon of Zeligism. This is not only a reference to the use of such testimony in Warren Beatty's *Reds* (1981) but also surely a joke at that overblown film's expense (as if Woody is consciously proving that he can make a much richer and more resonant movie than *Reds* at a third of the length, and in black and white, and *without* Diane Keaton). Intellectual celebrities such as Susan Sontag and Saul Bellow interpret Zelig's celebrity as

The fact is that no American film-maker had accomplished such a tour-de-force since Orsen Welles's *Citizen Kane* (1941), which shares this movie's fascination with film form, its skittishness toward 'March of Time' documentary, its labyrinthine search for the mystery of an ostensibly hollow personality. Like Welles's *F for Fake*, it raises charlatanism to an art, for it is a game played by a genius. As his name implies, Zelig seems alternatively silly and saintly, and this most cerebral and calculating of films nevertheless

Left: A ticker-tape welcome, à la Lindbergh, for Zelig and Eudora (Mia Farrow) in *Zelig.*

Below: Zelig's half-sister Ruth (Mary Louise Wilson) and her lover Martin Geist (Sol Lomita), who are to remove Zelig from the hospital and to exploit him as a sideshow freak.

symbolizing Jewish assimilation, human conformity, or the modern crisis of identity. He is all this and more, for *Zelig*, although a short movie, positively explodes with ideas. Zelig symbolizes the price of fame, where ecstasy can turn to excoriation overnight. As the ultimate conformist, he symbolizes the ultimate danger of conformity; it is the straight path to Fascism. Allen has said that Zelig is an embodiment of a 'minor malady that almost everyone suffers from – carried to an extreme.' He said once – it has been much quoted – that his one regret in life is that he is not someone else. In Zelig, he plays a man who is *everyone* else. Or maybe it is Woody Allen's go at the critics: they want him to be one thing, but *Zelig* is a film about a man who cannot stop shedding his skin. Or maybe the French have got it about right. 'French intellectuals', intones the narrator grandly, 'see him as a symbol for everything.'

Some critics grumbled about the film's relatively subdued humor, its fairly conventional romanticism (though this does not stop the love story of Zelig and Eudora being movingly played by Allen and Farrow) and that the technical wizardry is 'not worth it.'

also manages the most dazzling flights of imagination and has much to say about the human condition. *Zelig* is indeed a work of consummate artistry.

After the soaring ambition of *Zelig*, Woody once again kept his admirers off balance by following it with his most plot-oriented work since *Play It Again, Sam* and a reprise of the persona of lovable underdog. The loser is back. The eponymous hero of *Broadway Danny Rose* (1984), is a gentle theatrical agent who cares too deeply about his clients. He is a failure, representing other failures, with wit and kindness. Anyone who can make a sympathetic character out of an agent is probably made for life, and Danny Rose is one of Woody's most likeable roles.

It is not that the acts Rose represents lack talent. It is simply that they have limited appeal. They include a one-legged tap-dancer, a one-armed juggler, a balloon folder, an act that permits a skating penguin to do an impersonation of a rabbi, and a quite lethal hypnotist. ('If your wife never wakes up again,' Rose promises a comatose victim's distraught husband, 'I promise I'll take you to the restaurant of your choice'). Rose's main

Right: 'Star,' 'Smile,' 'Strong': agent Danny Rose advises ageing crooner, Lou (Nick Apollo Forte) in *Broadway Danny Rose.*

Below: Lou (Nick Apollo Forte) does his exuberant night-club routine in *Broadway Danny Rose.*

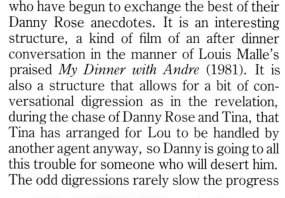

who have begun to exchange the best of their Danny Rose anecdotes. It is an interesting structure, a kind of film of an after dinner conversation in the manner of Louis Malle's praised *My Dinner with Andre* (1981). It is also a structure that allows for a bit of conversational digression as in the revelation, during the chase of Danny Rose and Tina, that Tina has arranged for Lou to be handled by another agent anyway, so Danny is going to all this trouble for someone who will desert him. The odd digressions rarely slow the progress of the film, which is one of Allen's most gripping narratives. It has some splendid set-pieces, notably the Mafia garden party which is thrown into chaos when Danny is fingered, and the usual adroit movie allusions, which include *Bicycle Thieves* (Tina is influenced by a lugubrious fortune-teller who seems straight out of the 1948 De Sica movie) and, of course, *The Godfather* (1972). Its combination of Mafia mirth and mayhem might also be said to anticipate the success of John Huston's black comedy which is along similar lines, *Prizzi's Honor* (1985).

The humor of *Danny Rose* is not black: more a sort of melancholy monochrome. A quick visual detail, like that shot in Danny's bathroom of three socks hanging up to dry, is funny but also an instant snapshot of his mental confusion and lonely bachelor status. At one stage of the film, Danny is cornered by the two thugs who have been chasing him. In desperation he names the world's worst ventriloquist Barney Dunn ('five-year-old kids would boo him') as Tina's lover, believing that Barney is safely away entertaining on a South American cruise. It is still something of a shock: Rose's falsely naming names out of

source of concern is an ageing, ambitious Italian crooner Lou (Nick Apollo Forte) who is having an affair with a girlfriend Tina (Mia Farrow) of a member of the Mafia. Rose's problems become desperate when he finds himself fingered as the girl's lover and becomes a target for the Mob.

The story of Danny Rose is narrated by one of a number of comedians who have gathered in the Carnegie Delicatessen Restaurant and

fear is a quick flashback to the McCarthyist atmosphere of *The Front*. In fact, Barney's cruise has been cancelled and, because of Danny's betrayal, he is badly beaten up. Danny's weight of guilt and sadness is instilled into a wonderfully gloomy shot of him as he leaves the Roosevelt Hospital in the rain after visiting the victim, and his contrition implied when we observe that an on-the-mend Barney is one of Danny's guests for Thanksgiving celebrations.

Most of all, the somberness beneath the comic sparkle derives not simply from plot quirks but from a characteristic scepticism about the American Dream. Less intense than *Stardust Memories*, *Broadway Danny Rose* is still a similarly thoughtful inquiry into the alienation rather than fulfillment of the American Dream, and what the pursuit and achievement of success can do to human relationships. (One is reminded of Elia Kazan's dictum that success is a bigger problem than failure, something with which Woody would surely agree). Perhaps the crucial scene in this regard is the one in which Danny learns of Lou's defection to another agent. It is the culmination of a previously cheerful conversation and conveyed in a stunning single take, the camera still as Danny and Lou approach, the tension of imminent disillusionment mounts, and the sickening revelation is delivered (and enlarged) at the precise moment when Danny comes into close-up.

In terms of characterization, *Danny Rose* is one of Woody Allen's warmest films. Much of its charm rests on the interaction between

Above: Danny Rose ruminates in a café, having just heard that a friend, Barney Dunn, has been beaten up by the Mob.

73

Above: Danny meets Lou's girlfriend, Tina (Mia Farrow), a blowsy blond with dubious Mafia connections.

Allen's resilient loser-hero and Mia Farrow's brassy broad. With his encouraging patter for his clients that is designed to launch them into the big time ('look in the mirror and say, "Star," "Smile," "Strong"'), his string of remembered philosophies from his 'completely dead' relatives (Uncle Sidney's 'Acceptance, Forgiveness, Love') and his verbal mannerisms ('may I interject one statement . . .'), Rose plays a completely rounded character,

and Allen plays him superbly. Even finer perhaps, because more unexpected, is Mia Farrow's tremendous performance as Tina, tough, fast-talking, widowed when her husband was shot in the eyes ('of course,' says Danny apprehensively, 'the bullets go right through') but still independent. Woody Allen grants her two sensational close-ups. The first is the moment when Danny meets her, as the door is opened and she bursts on the screen in the middle of an angry phone-conversation with Lou, and the photography tells it all about Danny's reaction: love at first sight. As in *Manhattan*, Woody will fall for the girl of his best friend. The second is the moment when she comes to Danny's apartment on Thanksgiving (an anticipation of *Hannah and Her Sisters*) and apologizes for her betrayal, and again the close-up tells it all: he is as much in love with her as ever. Danny is at first resentful and reserved, but he chases after her in the snow and, in a superbly timed sustained shot, catches up with her outside Carnegie's Delicatessen Restaurant – precisely the place where the story started. The pay-off is equally felicitous. Danny is immortalized by the restaurant's having named a sandwich after him – the Danny Rose special sandwich. It is a delicious movie, not perhaps his most substantial, but a delightful sweetener. The genial air is sustained by the appearance of some of Woody's comedian friends and heroes, like Milton Berle, and there are constant small delights, like, for example, that detail where Danny has no difficulty in freeing himself and Tina from the ropes of his captors; he has, after all, watched and managed an escape-act for years.

From Danny Rose to Purple Rose. Woody Allen's next movie is also about a whirlwind that comes into the life of a character's previous humdrum existence and also involves love at first sight. Also, as is characteristic of the later movies, the humor will be visual and conceptual more than verbal. The basic comic idea behind *The Purple Rose of Cairo* (1985) is nicely conveyed in that wan remark of Mia Farrow's depressed Depression housewife: 'I just met a wonderful new man – he's fictional, but you can't have everything.' The essence of the film is in that line: what happens when a film character, Tom Baxter (Jeff Daniels), steps from the screen into the housewife's real world; its theme of the tension between life and fiction; its tone of wondrous humor tinged with melancholy disillusionment. Screen escapism is rarely this delicate, this enchanting.

Escape, of one sort or another, is an important theme of the film. Monk (Danny

Above: Getting to know you: Danny learns of Tina's troubles in *Broadway Danny Rose.*

Left: Depression in America: Mia Farrow as a downtrodden thirties waitress and housewife in *The Purple Rose of Cairo.*

75

'My God, you must really love this picture,' says screen character Tom Baxter to the abashed spectator Cecilia and, to the consternation of both cast and audience, he suddenly walks out of the film and into the auditorium and whisks Cecilia away from the cinema. The remaining characters on the screen are as trapped as Buñuel's in *The Exterminating Angel* (1962): they cannot leave the film, yet the plot cannot proceed without the missing character. The audience is also disorientated: 'I just want what happened in the movie last week to happen again this week, otherwise what's life all about?' The studio is similarly affrighted by this possible threat of an actor's revolt – an ingenious reference to Hollywood history in the mid 1930s – and the ambitious young actor who plays Tom, Gil Shepherd, is dispatched

Above: Cecilia's husband, Monk (Danny Aiello, center) with his out-of-work cronies in *The Purple Rose of Cairo.*

Right: 'I want to be in pictures': Cecilia (Mia Farrow, center) is yanked into a movie by fugitive film character, Tom Baxter (Jeff Daniels, in the explorer's hat). From *The Purple Rose of Cairo.*

Far right: The poster for *The Purple Rose of Cairo.*

Aiello) escapes from the grinding boredom of unemployment in 1930s America by pitching pennies, playing dice, and chasing women. His wife Cecilia (Mia Farrow) forgets her troubles by going repeatedly to the cinema and losing herself in its magic. 'Heaven, I'm in Heaven . . .' are the first words we hear over the titles, crooned by Fred Astaire: it is the place where Cecilia is temporarily transported by movies, away from her unhappy marriage and her short-lived waitressing job with her sister (played by Mia Farrow's real-life sister, Stephanie). But what if the movie characters feel equally imprisoned and similarly long to escape the limitations of the film frame and the cramped imaginations of their creators?

to the cinema to sort out the situation. When told what has happened, Gil has cried, 'It's not physically possible,' but his agent is adamant: 'In New Jersey, anything can happen.'

Allen's inspiration for *Purple Rose* is not entirely new: Buster Keaton's *Sherlock Jr* (1924) did the situation in reverse when a projectionist dreams his way into the film he is projecting, and Federico Fellini's *The White Sheik* (1952) explores a relationship between a heart-throb actor and an adoring fan who are thrown unexpectedly together. What is fresh and original is the way Allen develops the idea. The 1930s film that Cecilia is watching and in which Tom is appearing, entitled 'The Purple Rose of Cairo' is a lovely take-off of RKO and Hollywood movie-making of the

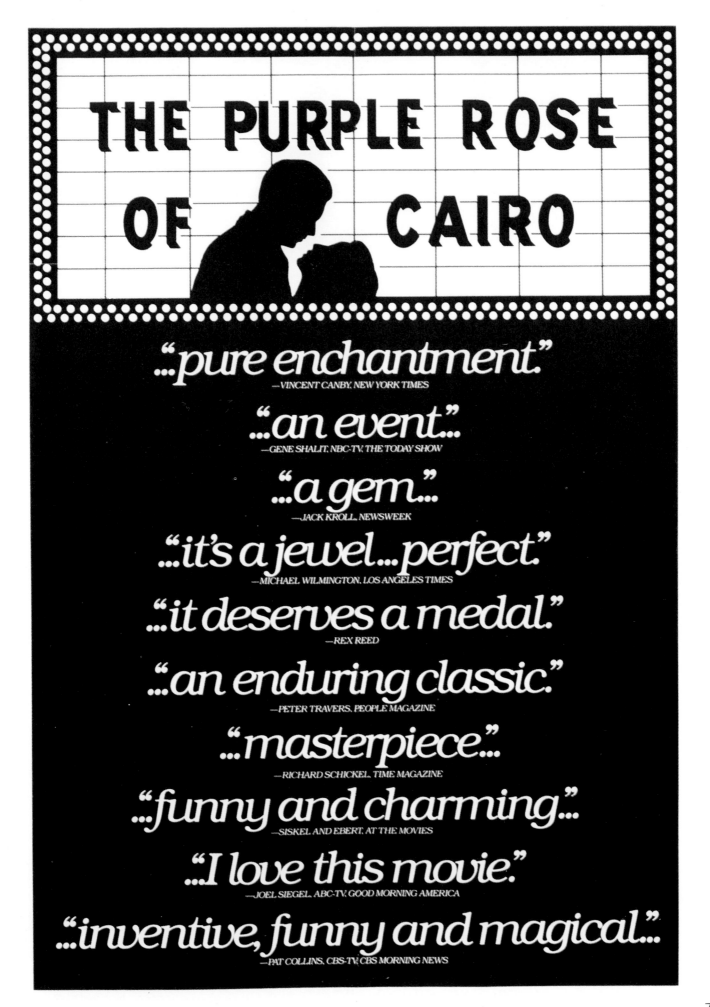

period, with actors and characters matching the old stars and styles of the past – John Wood in the Edward Everett Horton role, Milo O'Shea in the role of a priest that, in those days, would have gone to Pat O'Brien, and a black maid reminiscent of Hattie McDaniel's role in George Stevens's *Alice Adams* (1935). When Tom enters the real world – one of his first sights is the grim sign, 'Soup Kitchen' – he takes some time to adjust to its conventions. He expects screen money to be legal tender in a restaurant. He anticipates a fade-out after he has kissed Cecilia and, jumping into a car to make good an escape, wonders why it does not immediately start against a whirling backdrop. When he is lured to a brothel by the prostitute Emma, played by Dianne Wiest, he quite fails to grasp the nature of the place he is in, since movies of the

Above: Stranded in a movie: the characters in the film-within-a-film in *The Purple Rose of Cairo* anxiously await the return of the recalcitrant explorer – without him, their film cannot proceed.

Right: Mia Farrow as Cecilia in *The Purple Rose of Cairo*, with her hands on Depression dishes but her head in cinematic clouds.

Far right, above: Cecilia (Mia Farrow) finds herself attracted to the actor Gil Shepherd (Jeff Daniels) in *The Purple Rose of Cairo.*

Far right, below: Cecilia and Gil Shepherd in a scene from *The Purple Rose of Cairo.*

time mostly failed to acknowledge them also.

More variations are set in motion whcn Gil Shepherd comes to town. Jeff Daniels's dual performance is extremely skillful here, making a clear distinction between the genuinely innocent Tom and the ostensibly fresh-faced but actually calculating and ambitious Gil. Gil becomes drawn to Cecilia because she has seen all his films and acknowledges his versatility. In a clever modulation of the fantasy/reality theme, genuine romance between Gil and Cecilia begins to dawn when they begin instinctively to lapse into the dialogue of one of his movies (dialogue which Cecilia knows as well as Gil himself).

In a further variation, Tom returns to the movie but with Cecilia in tow, with the result that the scene of a madcap Manhattan weekend is entirely transformed: the night-club singer faints; the head-waiter is totally confused but takes the opportunity to break free from his constricted role by spontaneously bursting into an impromptu tap-dance routine

JEWEL

THE PURPLE ROSE OF CAIRO
R TALMADGE   RAYBURN   MORGAN

Where Hits are a Habit!

Above: Audiences gather outside a cinema, preparing to be taken out of their Depression blues.

which has always been his dream.

There is one particularly poignant detail in this revised night-club scene (which is delectably followed by a mock montage for their night out on the town). Cecilia notices that the champagne in this ostensibly stylish joint is actually ginger ale – a portent that her sparkling experience here is about to go flat. Forced to choose beween Tom and Gil, she chooses the latter, because he is real but, preparing to leave her husband for him, she discovers that Gil has flown back to Hollywood. 'Heaven, I'm in heaven ...' Slowly Cecilia wanders back into the cinema, her suitcase packed, but with nowhere else to go. Allen cuts between the movie screen and Cecilia's disconsolate face as she watches (she always seems to be looking *up* at people, and at life) and, through her changing expression, one senses the power of film magic to ease the pain of real life. It is a beautiful,

poignant conclusion: *Hannah and Her Sisters* will contain a similar scene, but the film extract in *Purple Rose* is better chosen for dramatic conviction and effect.

The technique is always exemplary: one fade from Cecilia's face to the screen action is a superb anticipation of how the real and the fantasy worlds in the movie will dissolve into each other. The color/black and white transitions for each shift of action between reality and fantasy are masterfully handled by cameraman Gordon Willis. The basic comic conceit is developed with great ingenuity. At times it is a Pirandellian game with six characters in search of an actor; at other times it is a philosophical sport in the style of Tom Stoppard, in which a character steps outside the dramatic fiction and muses about individual freedom and cinematic illusion, and in which a creator finds, like Dr Frankenstein, that his creation is getting out of control and

Left: Mia Farrow in *The Purple Rose of Cairo.* It was her fourth successive film with Woody Allen, and one of her most impressive and successful.

having a life of its own. There are a lot of references to other Allen movies: the familiar meditation on the difference and distance between Art and Life, and a sadness that life does not work out like movies; and the typical tone of sad romanticism, as both men lose the girl of their dreams and she must return to the prison of her marriage (both she and Tom Baxter are yearning for 'freedom – after two thousand performances').

Perhaps the domestic scenes are worked out with less freshness than the fantasy, but otherwise it is a gentle, generous film with a lovely central performance from Mia Farrow. Woody Allen does not himself appear, but his presence is felt, as the critic Robert Bena-youn has said, rather in the manner of the Cheshire Cat's invisible grin – appropriate for a movie with a logic and yet surreal imagination worthy of Lewis Carroll.

To borrow Woody Allen's liking for name-dropping, *Hannah and Her Sisters* (1986) is like a cross between Tolstoy's *Anna Karenina* and Bergman's *Fanny and Alexander* (1983) set to the music of Porter and Rodgers and Hart. Like the Tolstoy, which Woody Allen has said partly inspired the film, *Hannah* anatomizes an unhappy family and delights in the kind of narrative virtuosity which permits the tight interweaving of several different stories. Like the Bergman movie, *Hannah* is a large family saga that opens and closes on a festive family get-together and which, for all its darker passages, is ultimately affirmative in tone. The use of popular song in the film, as well as a Woody Allen trademark, comments meaningfully on the action, like, for example, the way 'You made me love you (I didn't wanna do it)' over the titles leads into Elliot's disclosure of his infatuation for his wife's sister. All in all, *Hannah and Her Sisters* is perhaps the most ambitious of Woody Allen's movies to date, with the largest canvas of important characters, and the longest running time (107 minutes). Whether this ambition is fully realized is, however, a moot point: it is a major movie without being quite the masterpiece a lot of critics have claimed.

The film begins at a Thanksgiving party, in which the characters are introduced and the surface harmony only thinly conceals the tensions beneath. Hannah (Mia Farrow), a semi-retired actress who has recently triumphed in *A Doll's House* is married to a financial adviser, Elliot (Michael Caine). However, Elliot's internal monologue discloses that he is in love with Hannah's sister, Lee (Barbara Hershey), who is having trouble in her relationship with an arrogant, cynical painter, Frederick (Max Von Sydow). Hannah's other sister, Holly (Dianne Wiest) is having career and character problems, but will later become emotionally involved with Hannah's ex-husband Mickey (Woody Allen),

a hypochondriac television producer who is first convinced that he has a brain tumor and then, when assured he has not, wonders afresh whether life has any meaning.

Perhaps the two Woody Allen films *Hannah* most immediately recalls are *Interiors* and *Manhattan*. Like *Interiors*, it is about the close but competitive relationship between three contrasting sisters and, as in the earlier film, the husband of one of the sisters makes a pass at one of his sisters-in-law (it is a curiously incestuous movie: Hannah's husband will fancy one sister while her ex-husband will marry another). Also like *Interiors*, the film studies the stormy relationship of the sisters' parents, finely played by Lloyd Nolan (his last film role) and Maureen O'Sullivan (who is Mia Farrow's actual mother, of course), who are either on

Far left, above: The Christmas dinner in Ingmar Bergman's *Fanny and Alexander*, a film which clearly had its influence on Allen's *Hannah and Her Sisters*.

Far left, below: The young children in Bergman's *Fanny and Alexander*.

Below: Intimations of mortality: Mickey receives some disturbing medical news in *Hannah and Her Sisters*.

each other's minds or at each other's throats. ('She got drunker and drunker and finally she became . . . Joan Collins!' says the father: Nolan delivers this line superbly). The main difference between *Hannah* and *Interiors* is one of tone, with *Hannah* treating its serious themes with an altogether lighter touch. Like *Manhattan*, *Hannah* is both set in, and a celebration of, New York, and deals with the confused love lives of the Manhattan middle-

class intelligentsia, who seem to know everything about the art of comfortable living but nothing about the complexity of their inner emotions. However, *Hannah* moves to a more upbeat conclusion than *Manhattan* and has a more objective tone, largely because, in *Hannah*, Woody Allen's part is more in the nature of a supporting role.

The theme of the film is encapsulated in two significant remarks. One is Elliot's to his

François Truffaut. The second important remark is Mickey's: 'The heart is a very, very resilient muscle.' Characters in Woody Allen's films take a rare emotional bruising but always seem to come back for more, and both Elliot and Mickey are ultimately to find some answers to the questions they find themselves asking about life and their emotions.

The performances are all first-rate, particularly Farrow, Hershey and Wiest as the three sisters. Woody Allen has become one of the cinema's great directors of actresses. Mia Farrow gives Hannah's seemingly invincible peaceful efficiency a poignantly precarious shell that sometimes seems about to break – her tremulous awareness during her parents' fierce argument of how beautiful they once were, her resentment at Holly's fiction which seems to be criticizing Hannah's marriage, her sense of Elliot's estrangement which gives her a sudden glimpse of the abyss ('so pitch black tonight – I feel lost', she says). Both her husband's affair and her sister's spiteful writing seem almost subconsciously inspired by their resentment of Hannah's 'perfection.' Barbara Hershey's performance as Lee movingly presents a vibrant, yet vulnerable personality lacking in self-confidence and seeming the prey of intellectually dominant men. As the ostensible 'loser' Holly, Dianne Wiest makes one feel the pathos behind the character's odd bouts of envy and despair. An argument between Hannah and Holly at a restaurant, while Lee sits tensely silent, is given additional tension by the claustrophobic, circling camerawork around the table and is one of the best scenes Woody Allen has ever directed.

Nevertheless, *Hannah* is a reminder that Woody Allen has never seemed very progressive in his attitude to women in his movies. He adores them, but does he really respect them? He loves their emotional generosity, but does he occasionally condescend to their intelligence? When Holly reads Mickey her new play, it is hard to tell from the evidence whether Mickey is genuinely impressed or just humoring her, and it is significant that two of the sisters are intellectually dependent on male approval for their own self esteem.

The male performances are all fine, though perhaps because of the characterization, less richly resonant than those of the women. Michael Caine is all menopausal melancholy, Woody Allen all harassed hypochondria, Max Von Sydow all artistic arrogance. Each of them is given at least one scene to display his talents at their finest. Caine is at his best when he is trying to break with Lee but is defeated and disorientated by her loving phone-call and just flounders momentarily in a

Hannah (Mia Farrow, left) and her sisters, Lee (Barbara Hershey, center) and Holly (Dianne Wiest, right).

analyst: 'For all my education and so-called wisdom, I can't fathom my own heart.' The character's perplexity over his adultery with Lee while still being in love with Hannah relates to Woody Allen's wider concern in all his work about the difficulty of love and the fragility of fidelity. His pain over the precariousness of the romantic couple, and the obsessiveness of sexual attraction, sometimes takes his cinema in the direction of

Above: Husband and wife reconciled at the end of *Hannah and Her Sisters*: Mia Farrow and Michael Caine.

sea of frustration and confusion. Von Sydow brings something of the power and anguish that one recalls from his Bergman performances. A scene where he describes an evening watching television, particularly the religious programs ('... If Jesus came back and saw what was going on in His Name, He wouldn't stop throwing up ...'), is funny on several levels – its portraiture of American TV, its reminder that Sydow himself played Christ in George Stevens's film, *The Greatest Story Ever Told* (1965) – but it is also gruellingly analytical and just too much for Lee. (It recalls Rita Hayworth's explanation for her divorce from Orson Welles: 'I just couldn't stand that man's genius'). Allen is at his best when worrying over his x-rays and particularly during a disastrous date with Holly, when she takes cocaine through the night-club act they attend and he loses hearing in one ear at the rock concert which is her treat for him.

Curiously, though, none of these characters is resolved very satisfactorily in dramatic terms. Elliot drifts back to his wife, lacking the courage to make any commitment to Lee, loving Hannah more than he thought, not

seeming to have learned much from his experience. True to life perhaps, but curiously anti-climatic as well. Frederick is written abruptly out of the narrative and his relationship with Lee is never that credible to begin with. After an anguished philosophical search in which he has lurched between Catholicism and Hare Krishna, Mickey finally decides life is worth living after laughing at the Marx Brothers in *Duck Soup*. Salvation through laughter is a nice idea but hardly an original one, having been done before in Preston Sturges's *Sullivan's Travels*, which Allen plagiarized much more inventively in *Stardust Memories*. The ending of *Purple Rose of Cairo* is also a more delicately and convincingly filmed example of the ability of movie fantasy to lance a person's private pain.

The comedy of *Hannah* is rather uneven. The montage of medical experiments on Mickey are funny but something of a stylistic break in tone and incongruously evoking the Allen of *Sleeper*. The line-up of targets is familiar – television, Freud, masturbation – but the famed one-liners seem sparse and less fresh than before. When Hannah and Mickey first learn that they cannot have children and she accuses him of 'excessive masturbation', he retorts: 'You gonna start knocking my hobbies?' It is a reasonable joke, but not as witty as Allen's definition of masturbation in *Annie Hall* – 'sex with someone I love' – and ultimately rather confused, for Holly is expecting Mickey's child at the end of the film, so what has happened to his supposed infertility?

Woody Allen could, of course, argue that he is dealing with less funny characters in *Hannah*. This is fair enough, and he is not to be blamed for the critical exaggeration about the film's supposed hilarity. But elsewhere the humor seems not simply subdued but rather labored. The film makes use of a reversal of expectations, but defeats the comic potential by making these reversals quite predictable. For example, when Elliot counsels himself to be cautious when approaching Lee, you know that the next moment he will be grabbing her violently and kissing her. When Mickey tells himself not to panic over his suspected illness, you can predict that the next shot will show his waking up in the night and shouting, in panic, 'I'm dying!' The jokes are not bad, just obvious. Less obvious, but more dubious, are the frequent references to Nazism and the Holocaust for comic effect. When he made a sick joke about the extermination of Jews in *Stardust Memories* ('If I had been born in Poland, or Berlin, I'd be a lampshade today'), it seemed totally in keeping with the bitterness of the character and the savagery of the film. When he does it in *Hannah* ('I had a great time tonight,' Mickey tells Holly after their disastrous date, 'it was like the Nuremberg trials!') it seems rather discordant and out of character. Again one could argue that Mickey is obsessed with Nazism in his quest for the meaning of life, but why does Frederick also refer to it ('You missed a dull TV show on Auschwitz tonight') and even Elliot (when likening his wife's questioning to 'the Gestapo')? The impression given is less that of a meaningful metaphor than that of a poverty of imagination.

The structure too is an odd mixture of deftness and dexterity and archness and awkwardness. The flashbacks are cunningly inserted; it is intriguing that the three women constantly meet yet the three men hardly ever meet; and there are all kinds of neat parallels and seemingly stray details that bind the material together (the abyss that links Hannah and Mickey at different stages, the *Weltschmerz* that unexpectedly unites Mickey and Frederick). Yet the titles that punctuate the episodes seem derivative (of Billy Wilder's 1966 film *The Fortune Cookie*) and

unnecessary, while the interior monologues are used less for intriguing self-revelation than for obvious narrative signposting. We should not need to be told so baldly by the narration that Lee is Hannah's sister, that Mickey is Hannah's ex-husband, that Lee has a new boyfriend: such details should emerge organically from the material itself.

Much of the appeal of the movie depends on how the individual spectator responds to the characters and to their embodiment of the neurotic charms of the bourgeoisie. Are not their problems a little remote from most of us, and the resolution of these problems a little pat and complacent? *Hannah* sometimes gives the impression of a party for old friends hosted by the director, with uncredited 'surprise' appearances from members of the Woody Allen repertory company, like Sam Waterston and Tony Roberts, and with the audience given the uncomfortable impression that it should feel privileged even to be there. One is undoubtedly impressed by the quality

Below: Mickey and Hannah (Mia Farrow) discuss their problems in *Hannah and Her Sisters*, on learning that they cannot have children.

of mind at work (one recalls the hero's referring to the brain as 'my second favorite organ' in *Sleeper*): at the same time, the suggestion of conceitedness is a little disconcerting. Overall, *Hannah and Her Sisters* seems less thematically challenging than *Stardust Memories*, less technically adventurous than either *Zelig* or *The Purple Rose of Cairo*, and soft-centered and sentimental beneath its sophistication and subtlety.

CHAPTER FOUR

GENTLE GENIUS

Page 88: Woody Allen lines up a shot for *Everything You Always Wanted to Know About Sex.*

It is a critical commonplace nowadays to discuss the gentle (not gentile) genius of Woody Allen in terms of Jewish humor. This traditionally takes the form of comparing him with fellow Jewish performers and directors like Groucho Marx, Mel Brooks and Billy Wilder and widening the perspective to include contemporary American writers to whom the Jewish experience has been germinal, like Saul Bellow, Joseph Heller and Philip Roth. Woody Allen's comedy is thus discussed in terms of what are defined as primary characteristics of Jewish humor: the aggression of Groucho Marx or Wilder, or Lenny Bruce, or the self-deprecation, paranoia and guilt that is more marked in Woody Allen's own work, as in the bad taste joke in *Stardust Memories*, and the early conversation in *Annie Hall* where Alvy seems determined to confuse an overheard 'Did you?' with the muttered imprecation, 'Jew.'

There are two immediate qualifications one would make to this categorization of Allen's humor. Firstly, it is too America-oriented: one could equally see Allen in a tradition of European Jewish art in which he shares

something of the gallows humor of Franz Kafka, and particularly shares the emotional intensity of a Gustav Mahler who, for all his sardonic irony, cannot disguise his deeply felt romanticism. Allen's romanticism, though, is a reminder of the second reservation about this 'Jewish humor' label: that it is simply too limiting to contain all of his complexity. In many ways, the artist he resembles most would be Scott Fitzgerald (who, one might recall, is the person who first spots Leonard Zelig at that Long Island party). Zelig is as mysterious, elusive and magnetic as Jay Gatsby; Allen's heroes often have something of the make-up of Dick Diver in Fitzgerald's *Tender is the Night*, where civilized wisdom is sometimes undermined by romantic vulnerability. Like Scott Fitzgerald, Woody Allen's characters have emotional not financial problems, and brittle, tortured, relationships are enacted against a background of empty stultifyingly affluence.

His movies have sometimes been criticized for their bourgeois angst, which, to some, seems narcissistic and indeed irrelevant in a world of poverty, recession and violence. Yet

Below: Woody Allen, as crumpled idealist, and Andrea Markovicci as his girlfriend, in Martin Ritt's *The Front.*

it would be unfair to criticize him for an absence of political or social commitment. Indeed the message of his films, no less strong because it is oblique, can be interpreted as a powerful indictment of an America whose massive resources contrast tragically with its cultural poverty. This critique is expressed in Allen's films through his open bold contempt for Los Angeles society and his preference for New York. Even more, it is expressed in the kind of movies he makes, which are adult, literate and structured.

Too much of modern mainstream American film (*Cobra, Top Gun*) displays a mindless violence that almost brings to mind that famous utterance of Hermann Goering: 'When I hear the word "culture", I reach for my gun.' Woody Allen's cinema brings to mind Cyril Connolly's response to the Goering statement: 'When I hear the word "gun", I reach for my culture.' Against the fashions of the time but in the tradition of the great writer-directors of the American cinema like Preston Sturges, Joseph Mankiewicz and

Above: Martin Ritt (right) directs *The Front*, while Woody Allen sits attentively.

Left: Diane Keaton receives the Oscar for Best Actress for her performance in the title role of *Annie Hall*. Woody won his for writing and directing but predictably did not turn up at the ceremony.

Billy Wilder, he has insisted on the primacy of wit and intelligence over sensationalism as the prerequisites of good popular cinema. The intellectualism is not self-advertisement so much as self-defense against encroaching barbarism. When he mentions Ibsen, Nietzsche, Tolstoy and Socrates in *Hannah and Her Sisters*, one feels he is not simply telling us he has read these people. He is genuinely afraid that, in a technocratic society characterized by visual saturation and verbal illiteracy, such cultural giants are in danger of being forgotten.

The fact that Woody Allen has nevertheless been able to air and debate such feelings within popular cinema is both a tribute to popular cinema's range and flexibility and also to Allen's own cunning. He has never been a profligate director, so that his films, if not blockbusters, have never lost money and, in the case of *Annie Hall* and *Hannah and Her Sisters*, have made a substantial profit. Because of this, he has attracted little interference and the industry has tended to leave him alone. Over the years, he has become a sort of one-man industry, and a recognizable Woody Allen repertory company has begun to form. Diane Keaton, Tony Roberts and more recently, Mia Farrow have become the stalwart Allen performers. Gordon Willis has been his regular cameraman, with the odd exception like *Hannah and Her Sisters* which was photographed by Carlo di Palma. Mel Bourne has been his usual art director; Dick Hyman his most trusted composer. Ralph Rosenblum edited all the movies up to and including *Manhattan*; Susan Morse all the movies after that. Mickey Rose and Marshall Brickman have been his most regular co-writers, though since *Manhattan*, Woody has written all his own screenplays. Even his

Above: Ingmar Bergman at work. Bergman is Allen's favorite director and has had an increasing influence on his work since *Love and Death*.

Left: Woody discusses a scene in *The Purple Rose of Cairo* with Mia Farrow, who has become one of his most important performers and has appeared in his last five films.

Far left: Woody Allen and Diane Keaton, romantic partners in *Play It Again, Sam*.

advertising has become distinctive: generally modest, subdued and more quietly personal than is customary in the industry.

Equally remarkably, he has achieved three things which are almost impossible in the climate of today's cinema. Firstly, he has been prolific. He has succeeded in sustaining an average of a film a year at a time when other talented directors are struggling to achieve any continuity in their careers. Secondly, he has been unpredictable. Rather than follow the trends of his own and other people's successes, he has kept audiences and critics guessing, through the sheer variety of his work. Every new film seems different from the one that preceded it. Thirdly, he has been consistent. Despite ringing the changes and despite being so productive, he has somehow managed to sustain a level of interest and excellence that has scarcely any parallel in the cinema of the 1980s. Has any other director made half-a-dozen films over the same period of the level of Allen's work since *Manhattan*?

A note on the dust jacket of a recent publication on Woody Allen claims: 'No one before him had extracted humor from sub-jects like death, suicide, and the difficulty of existence'. This is not strictly true, of course; what about Chaplin, and Billy Wilder? In fact, the note inadvertently reminds us that Woody Allen has not the social rage and range of a Chaplin nor the moral tight-rope-walking skill of a Wilder; that he has not yet made a great black comedy; and that his definitive master-piece is probably still to come. His originality lies elsewhere: in his combination of comedy with philosophy; his technical audacity; his unusual persona of a clown with a genuine romantic idealism and a considerable intellect; and his bold expression of some of the dis-satisfactions of the American Dream of wealth and fame. More than any other contemporary personality, he has come to embody the witty man's burden; the knowledge that the modern world is mad and meaningless and that our sanity and survival might depend on our capacity to make it appear merely comically mistaken. The annual Woody Allen movie has become one of the most important dates on the calendar for anyone who cares about cinema and its development, and about civili-zation and its discontents.

Below: Woody Allen and the telephone as life-line in *Play It Again, Sam.*

Right: The serious face of comedy, Woody Allen, who once said, 'I don't want to achieve immortality through my work, I want to achieve it through not dying.'

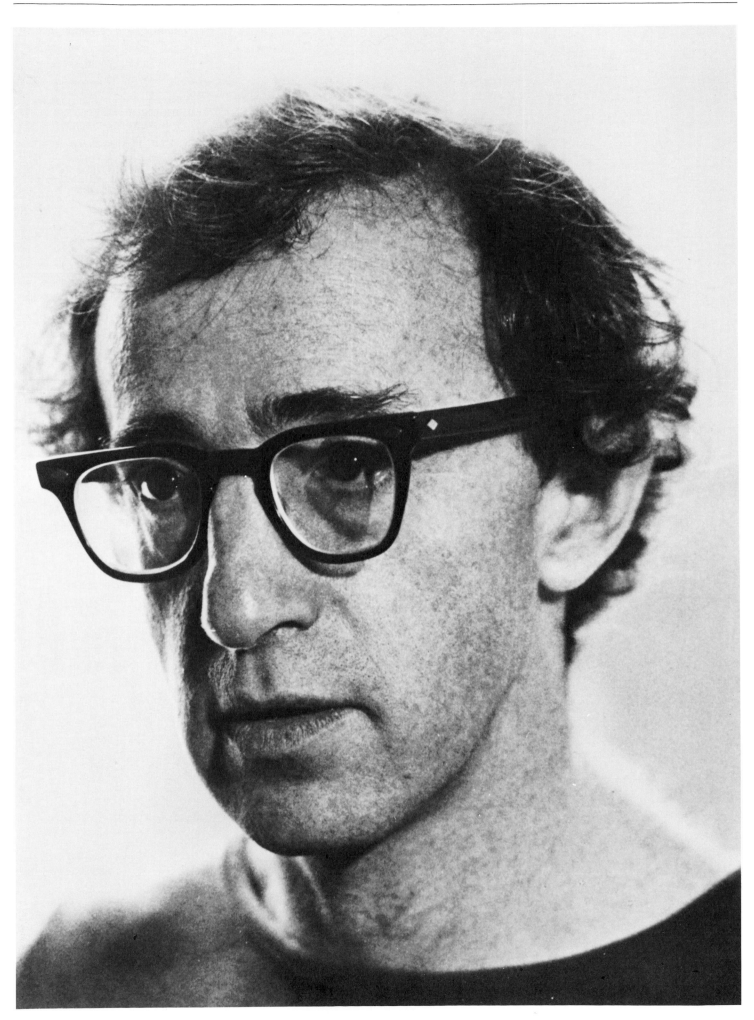

Index

Page numbers in *italics* refer to illustrations. Page numbers in **bold** refer to major coverage of a film.

Acknowledgments

The publisher would like to thank the following people who helped in the preparation of this book: Design 23, who designed it; Wendy Sacks, who edited it; Mandy Little, who carried out the picture research; and Ron Watson, who compiled the index. Our thanks, too, to the National Film Archive, London, who supplied all the illustrations except for the following:

Academy of Motion Picture Arts and Sciences: pages 17, 22 (top), 49 (top), 54 (bottom), 62, 91 (top), 95.
BBC Hulton Picture Library: page 1.
Joel Finler: pages 13 (bottom), 14, 19, 21 (bottom), 26 (top), 38 (top and bottom), 39 (top), 46 (bottom), 47 (top), 50 (bottom).
Jerry Ohlinger: pages 10 (bottom), 12 (top and bottom), 68 (bottom), 83, 84-5, 86, 87.